Ripley's Believe It or Not!

Special Edition 2014

SCHOLASTIC INC.

ISBN 978-0-545-56647-6

PUBLISHING

Developed and produced by Ripley Publishing Ltd

Publisher: Anne Marshall
Editorial Director: Becky Miles
Art Director: Sam South

Editor: Rosie Alexander
Project Editor: Charlotte Howell
Senior Researcher: James Proud
Design: Rocket Design (East Anglia) Ltd
Indexer: Hilary Bird
Reprographics: Juice Creative

Cover credits:
China Foto Press/Photocome/Press Association Images
12 11 10 9 8 7 6 5 4 3 2 1   13 14 15 16 17 18/0

Printed in China   62
First Printing, September 2013

Page
125

Page 115

Page 76

Contents

Page 139

Meeow

Meeow

Page 72

Page 126

Welcome to Ripley's!

"That's one for Ripley's" is a phrase entering everyday speech. Everyone knows what it means: It's life when it's really and truly extraordinary. Use it to refer to a curious critter, an incredible invention, or a fabulous feat—something that makes us grimace and gasp, and everything else in between. But don't use it too often—it should describe just the very best!

Robert Ripley sparked off the Ripley phenomenon in 1918, when he started work at the *New York Globe* newspaper as a cartoonist, and made it his aim to reveal the world's most unbelievably true stories. He traveled the world, covering 464,000 miles in his lifetime, hand-picking the finest material for his cartoons.

In 1933, Ripley opened a museum—called an Odditorium —for the strange things he collected. He threw himself into radio and television, broadcasting his weird findings from wild locations—behind Niagara Falls for example—and thrilling his audience until it was claimed that he was more popular than the US president.

Ripley searches through his boxes of mail.

That's Ripley Pushing!

Robert Ripley went to great lengths to find the perfect story, traveling in Russia in 1933 where he had to get yaks to pull his car out of a snowdrift.

4

The first Ripley's museum opened in Chicago, in 1933, to much acclaim.

A brand-new one opened in Baltimore last year!

The Believe It or Not! cartoons, originally drawn by Robert Ripley, below in 1931, are still published daily.

BELIEVE IT OR NOT—By Ripley
(Copyright. 1930)

THE FIVE-WAY WORD!
5 DIFFERENT WAYS OF SPELLING
5 DIFFERENT MEANINGS —

HEIR—INHERITOR, SUCCESSOR
AIR — THE ATMOSPHERE
AYR—A SAND-BANK
ERE —BEFORE—ERE DAYLIGHT
E'ER—EVER, WHATE'ER, ETC

THE BOWER BIRDS —of Australia BUILD HUTS AND KEEP GARDENS

SHARED SAME BED BUT SLEPT IN DIFFERENT STATES THE WALLACES, of Claremore LIVED EXACTLY ON THE GEORGIA-TENNESSEE LINE

A REAL H.E. MANN — of Memphis CAN CARRY — not throw A 600-POUND BULL

IN MEMORY OF WILLIAM REDSDALE DIED FEBRUARY 30th 1802

A STONE IN THE VILLAGE OF FEWSTON, Eng.

Fans sent Ripley 3,000 letters a day—each one supplying him with a fun fact or shocking story. Today, our fans keep in touch through e-mail, Facebook, and Twitter. Twelve million visitors pass through the turnstiles at our 31 museums in 11 different countries each year. With so many people happily involved in our Ripley world, is it any wonder "that's one for Ripley's" is now street speak?

5

It's a Big, Wild World!

Ripley archivist, Edward Meyer, based at our Florida HQ, hunts tirelessly for new artifacts to put in our museums, whether it involves bidding at organized sales, rummaging through old private collections, or unexpectedly jumping onto planes to secure exhibits. Some of Edward's stories are as incredible as the items he finds. . . .

Captain America built from car parts by a company in Thailand.

"We once discovered a stuffed albino moose in a bar in Cochrane, Canada. We offered to buy the whole bar, because we wanted the moose so badly, but couldn't make a deal. Many years later, the owner phoned me out of the blue and we bought the moose!"

"The Lord's Prayer carved on the head of a small hatpin was first displayed at the Chicago World's Fair in 1894 and again in 1933—then it disappeared. I found it one cold, rainy day in Seattle, Washington, in 1989, in a small envelope in a shoebox, while looking through a collection of 30,000 uncatalogued miniatures."

Look what Ripley's bought this year!

A clownfish made from deflated balloons by James Perry from Michigan.

Molly B. Right's bottle-top portrait of Michelle Obama.

From cover to cover, this book is bursting with amazing pictures and reports.....

Keep an eye out for the Ripley interviews!

Think spot!
Splat! Another fascinating fact crash-lands.

On pages 40–41 and 112–113, we've opened the Ripley's vaults and pulled out photographs from the 25,000 images we have on file!

See page 54

See page 48

If you have a story you think Ripley's would like, get in touch!

Visit our website
www.ripleybooks.com
E-mail us bionresearch@ripleys.com
Follow us on Facebook and Twitter @RipleyWorld
Write to BION research, Ripley Entertainment Inc., 7576 Kingspointe Parkway, Suite 188, Orlando, Florida 32819

And include photos if you can!

Check out another Believe It or Not! story when you turn the page!

World Exclusive

chapter 1

Weather... or Not

Ghostly Rainbow

In the monochrome world of the Arctic, it seems that even the rainbows are white. This rare phenomenon, spotted by the crew of an icebreaker ship, is called a *fogbow*. It's formed in the same way as a rainbow, but the tiny water droplets that make up fog are too small to separate light into rainbow colors.

Crafted by Nature

In February 2012, strange, skirtlike ice formations were found attached to tree trunks in the Lower Oder Valley National Park, on the border between Germany and Poland. The icy adornments glinted in the winter sun like beautiful crystal chandeliers.

Cloud Creator

Berndnaut Smilde from Amsterdam, Holland, uses a smoke machine combined with moist air to produce indoor clouds. Dramatic backlighting creates shadows to give the impression of a typical Dutch rain cloud floating within an empty hall. Unlike real rain clouds, these soon disappear, so the artist relies on photographs to preserve the eerie image.

Think spot!

Earthworms rained down on students playing soccer in Scotland! Freak weather over a nearby river lifted the water and worms, and dropped them there.

Unidentified Flying Cloud

It's not surprising that people sometimes claim to have spotted a UFO after seeing a lenticular cloud. These spaceship-shaped clouds have smooth edges and appear to hover. They are usually formed when high winds force moist air up a hill or mountain and the moisture condenses in the cooler air above the summit, creating a cloud.

Landscape Painting

Toxic Beauty

The Wujiang River, which flows through China's Guizhou Province, is a stunning peacock blue but, sadly, the water's extraordinary color is the result of pollution. Agricultural and industrial waste, combined with poor sewage systems, threaten both the fish and the safety of the local water supply.

Think spot!

The Pasig River in the Philippines flows both ways. The direction varies according to the water level in the lake at its source.

Putting Art on the Map

Michael Wallace's paintbrush is his mountain bike and his canvases are GPS maps of Baltimore, Maryland. The science teacher sketches an interesting design by following the city streets, then he hops on his bike and traces out the route. He uses a GPS tracker to "draw" the images, which include monsters, animals, and even a map of the US.

Pretty in Pink

British artist Henry Bruce has painted a skeletal 70-foot-tall tree shocking pink to make people aware of a destructive fungus that is killing trees. The pink-painted oak on the grounds of the Delamore Estate, in southwest England, is part of an annual art and sculpture exhibition.

Living Walls

Nikita Nomerz brings abandoned buildings back to life by turning them into quirky characters. On their walls, the Russian street artist paints faces that laugh, scream, or simply stare at passersby with their broken-window eyes. He started out as a typical hip-hop graffiti artist before deciding to give run-down structures a face-lift.

What's unfolding?
Flick to page 63 to see more!

Vacation of a Lifetime

Courageous Kayakers

Three daredevil kayakers paddled to the edge of Victoria Falls in southern Africa just to take a closer look at the largest waterfall in the world. No one has ever survived the sheer 350-foot drop, but that was not the only danger they faced, because the waters at the top are home to crocodiles and hippos. Once they had taken in the view, South Africans Steve Fisher and Dale Jardine and American Sam Drevo rappelled down with their kayaks and successfully navigated the wild waters below!

INTERVIEW

Dale, did you have to meticulously plan your route or was it a spur-of-the-moment thing?

I lived in Victoria Falls for ten years and in that time no one ever paddled up to the edge, so we planned our route as best we could. Steve and I both worked as guides above and below the Falls for many years so we knew too well the dangers around us, such as the hippos above the Falls! Our experience as professional kayakers made it easier, but that's not to say that we weren't nervous. We always made sure we could get to a safe point where we would be able to get out before being in any danger.

What was it like peering over the edge?

It was awesome in every sense of the word; the magnificent power of the forces of nature were overwhelming. The noise of the wind was so tremendous that we could hardly hear each other; it gave me shivers down my spine.

Was it worth all the danger? If yes, in what way?

Most definitely! When you are there, all the danger goes away and you live in the moment. To be able to do something that not many people will ever get to experience makes it a unique opportunity, and I would do it again tomorrow if I could!

Hot Dinner

Hotel Holt in Iceland offered guests a unique outdoor dining experience right next to a spewing volcano. Despite the glowing lava, temperatures were well below freezing when the diners arrived by helicopter. Luckily, they did not have long to wait for their meal—chefs prepared dinner on the freshly erupted lava, which, at close to 350°F, cooked the food in record time.

Think spot!

Buddhist monk Endo Mitsunaga walked 26 miles a day around Mount Hiei, Japan, for 1,000 days, which is equivalent to walking once around the Earth.

Cool Hotel

Each winter, when Balea Lake in central Romania freezes over, local craftsmen drag blocks of ice up the mountain to carve the Ice Hotel. The temperature inside the hotel hovers around zero and guests sleep on ice beds with reindeer fur blankets. In the restaurant, diners sit on fur-lined ice chairs at ice tables and drink from glasses made of ice.

Travel Companions

Human Camera

Photographer Tyler Card's Halloween costume not only looks like a Nikon DSLR camera, it actually functions as one! Tyler from Grand Rapids, Michigan, used a five-gallon bucket, a cardboard box, and a piece of Plexiglas® to create his costume, then he put his own camera in the lens and attached a laptop to serve as the viewfinder.

Breath of Fresh Air

Nanning in southern China is known as the "Green City" because of its lush tropical foliage. Now people in Nanning and outside the city can enjoy the scent of the great outdoors without leaving home by buying a jar of fresh air collected from the forest. The jars cost $2.80 each.

Say cheese!

良凤江清新空气
18元/瓶

Supersized Deck Chair

British sculptor Stuart Murdoch marked the start of Daylight Saving Time by erecting a 28-foot-tall deck chair on Bournemouth Beach, on England's south coast. It took three weeks to build and, because it weighs more than an adult elephant, there is no danger of it blowing away in the wind.

Sunny-Side Up

According to her owner, Rosie the hen from Maidenhead, England, can foretell the weather through her eggs. An egg with white speckles warns of snow, while one clean white egg followed by one with orange spots forecasts clear skies and sunny spells. Two sunny days were predicted by eggs with marks in the shape of a shining sun.

Think spot!

When shopping in Japan, it's considered rude to place money in the hands of a cashier.

17

PROOF OF EVIDENCE

Sssss!

ROCK SCHOOL

Villagers in a mountain area of Guizhou, one of China's poorest provinces, could not afford to build a school, so they set up classrooms in a huge cave instead. Bats made biology a hands-on experience!

FORTUNE FROM FANGS

There are about 8,500 snakes for each person in the farming village of Zisiqiao in China's Zhejiang Province. Families there earn money from breeding snakes, including cobras, vipers, and pythons, for use in food or traditional medicine, and as a tourist attraction.

BRAVE BOATMAN

When a tsunami hit the Japanese island of Oshima in 2011, most people fled to the hills, but Susumu Sugawara steered his boat out to sea. The 64-year-old rode waves 60 feet tall and his was the only surviving vessel able to help for weeks afterward.

POP-UP CROSSING

A frustrated father created his own pedestrian crossing after the Highway Authority refused to install a real one outside his son's school in Kingston upon Thames, England. Yannick Read made the makeshift crossing, which can be put up and removed in one minute, using recycled flooring material, with painted drainpipes and yellow balloons as beacons.

COLD SNAP

After photographer Yuri Ovchinnikov's son put his foot through the ice of the Tianuksa River in Russia, Yuri put his camera in the hole and took photos of caverns formed by pockets of air.

Woahhh!

FREEZE FRAMES

Italian photographer Niccolò Bonfadini spent nine days camping alone in Finnish Lapland to capture images of the Arctic Circle's surreal terrain. As temperatures dropped to −40°F, everything was engulfed in solid ice, including the trees, which resembled ghostly aliens rising from an otherworldly landscape.

NEED A NAP?

Tired travelers stuck at Moscow's Sheremetyevo Airport can now rest their weary heads on something more comfortable than a terminal bench. Self-contained Sleepboxes can be rented for 30-minute periods and contain bunk beds, a fold-out desk, and space for luggage.

ERUPTING SPORT

Thrill seekers are heading for Nicaragua's 2,380-foot-tall Cerro Negro to take part in the extreme sport of volcano boarding, reaching speeds of up to 50 mph.

ROOM FOR REFLECTION

The 4,000-square-mile Salar de Uyuni salt pan in Bolivia is so flat that rain cannot drain away. Instead, it creates a sheet of water to form the world's largest natural mirror.

SINKING FEELING

When Inocenta Hernandez was woken by a massive crash, she thought a gas canister had exploded, but instead the grandmother from Guatemala discovered that a 40-foot-deep, 3-foot-wide sinkhole had suddenly appeared in the floor.

FESTIVE FIR

Each year, volunteers from the Italian town of Gubbio spend three months stringing more than 28,000 feet of cables and 800 lights up the slope of Mount Ingino to create a dazzling, 2,130-foot-tall installation in the shape of a Christmas tree. The shining silhouette, which towers above the medieval city, can be seen from more than 30 miles away.

TORNADO TERROR

In April 2011, the southern United States was devastated by a deadly series of tornados, including at least four with the most powerful EF5 ranking. On April 27, a total of 226 tornados were reported during a single 24-hour period.

Watery Brave

Jellyfish Soup

Most swimmers head swiftly in the opposite direction when they spot a jellyfish, so why would people flock to snorkel alongside ten million moon jellies and golden jellyfish? Jellyfish Lake on the Pacific island Eil Malk has been cut off from the sea for many years and, because they have no predators, the jellies' stings have become so weak they cannot harm humans.

Think spot!

No one retrieves lost balls from the golf course lake in Carbrook, Australia. After a flood in the 1990s, it became home to a group of dangerous bull sharks.

Call the Coast Guard

Julien Berthier's crazy sculpture is so convincing that good Samaritans often come to his aid. The French artist created his capsizing yacht, christened *Love Love*, by cutting a boat in half and adding a new keel so it stays upright in the sinking position. The craft is actually seaworthy—it has an onboard motor and has toured around Europe.

Natural Wonder

With an average thickness of 1,310 feet, Vatnajökull in Iceland is the largest glacier in Europe. Beneath the surface where it meets the coast, a breathtaking crystal cave has formed. Inside, the awesome force of the glacier has forced all the air out of the ice, turning it a stunning sapphire blue.

Daring Dip

Hot tubs are normally all about relaxation, but perhaps not if you are dangling 500 feet above the Trient Gorge in Switzerland. A group of 25 extreme hot-tub fanatics spent six hours suspending a makeshift tub from the Gueuroz Bridge, before rappelling onto the platform to enjoy a couple of hours hanging out in the bubbling water.

RIPLEY RECORDS

▶ **DEEPEST ASSISTED (WITH A PROPELLED SLED) FREE DIVE** Herbert Nitsch from Austria took a single gulp of air and plunged to 800 feet in 2012. At depths over 164 feet, lungs fill with pink, frothy blood plasma, the heart slows to 15 beats a minute, and, with no goggles, eyeballs would be sucked out.

▶ **DEEPEST FREE DIVE WITHOUT MECHANICAL ASSISTANCE** With one breath, in June 2012, Will Trubridge swam 331 feet 4 inches down and back.

▶ **LONGEST HELD BREATH** In May 2012, German Tom Sietas held his breath underwater for 22 minutes 22 seconds, a world record.

▶ **DEEPEST OCEAN** At 6.831 miles down, Challenger Deep, in the Pacific Ocean east of the Philippines, is the world's deepest point in the ocean. Pressure there is the same as the weight of 50 jumbo jets pressing down on a human body.

We're here!

What's unfolding? Flick to page 115 to see more!

Crazy Countryside

Pylon People

For many, these towerlike structures used for carrying power lines are a blot on the landscape. But pylons have their fans, including members of the Pylon Appreciation Society and those who post pictures on the Pylon of the Month website. This design, proposing giant humanoid pylons, was submitted by US architects Choi+Shine for Iceland's High-Voltage Pylon Competition.

Think spot!

A signpost in Lynchville, Maine, points to Paris (15 miles), Denmark (23 miles), Mexico (37 miles), and China (94 miles). They are all the names of local towns.

Beam Me Up

Perfect for sci-fi fans, the latest addition to Sweden's Treehotel looks just like a UFO. Visitors can enjoy their own close encounter in Swedish Lapland, where the hotel has a number of individually designed rooms suspended in the treetops near Harads. The retro flying saucer has two stories and space for four alien fans.

Cunning Camouflage

During World War II, the Lockheed Vega aircraft plant in Burbank, California, was hidden successfully beneath a huge tarp painted with rural neighborhood scenes to protect it from a Japanese air attack. Hundreds of fake trees and shrubs were created from chicken wire and painted feathers, buildings were positioned to give a 3-D appearance, and air ducts were disguised as fire hydrants. Rubber automobiles were moved daily and laundry was taken down and replaced on fake clotheslines.

Back to Nature

Briny Beauty

Microorganisms in the salt ponds on the shores of San Francisco Bay in California produce dramatic colors, ranging from pale green to deep coral pink, depending on the amount of salt in the water. Low salt levels favor green algae, while red algae thrive in a high salt environment. Millions of tiny brine shrimp living in medium-salty ponds give the water an orange hue.

Think spot!

If you travel directly north, south, east, or west from Stamford, Connecticut, you will enter the state of New York.

Crazy Cascade

Disposing of old bathroom furniture can be a problem, so why not recycle it as a garden water feature? This 328-foot-long waterfall is made from 10,000 toilets and washbasins. The bizarre art project was on display in a park in Guangdong Province, China, as part of a trade show for pottery and porcelain products.

Rocky Horror

Hodge Close Quarry in the English Lake District can be a scary place, and its underwater cave system has claimed the lives of several divers. Photographer Peter Bardsley captured this chilling image after diving at the remote site. It was only after processing the photo and turning it sideways that he noticed the skull-shaped face created by the reflection on the water.

Water World

Using large satellite photos of the Earth as backgrounds, Markus Reugels from Germany manages to capture the images through a droplet of falling water to create a perfect mini-world. Reugels began taking photographs as a hobby after his son was born and it soon turned into a passion, leading to his beautiful experimental photographs using water droplets.

MAXIMIZE

Hot Shots

Carsten Peter endured temperatures of over 2,000°F to capture these awe-inspiring images from the mouths of two of the world's most dangerous volcanos. The intrepid German photographer accompanied scientists collecting lava samples from Mount Etna on the Italian island of Sicily, then rappelled into the fiery crater of Nyiragongo, which towers over the Democratic Republic of Congo. Although Carsten wore a heat protection suit, his life was still at risk from toxic gases, rockfalls, and "lava bombs."

Mount Etna is Europe's tallest active volcano and has been erupting regularly from its present center for about 170,000 years.

Mount Nyiragongo in the Rift Valley is the most active volcano in Africa. Its 3,900-foot-wide crater contains one of the largest lakes of molten lava on Earth.

In a Town Near You

Sock Yarn

Knitters from more than ten countries made baby socks as part of a project organized by a German wool manufacturer. A total of 12,262 pairs were collected at the International Opal Sock Knitters' Meeting in Hechingen, Germany, and clipped to a clothesline 4,231 feet long. The socks were donated to charity organizations after the event.

Secret Door

Joe Pires's Florida home has a full-width porch with windows and decorative shutters, a table and chairs, and a functioning front door, but it also has a surprise in store. At the push of a button, the entire porch swings up to reveal a hangar large enough for a full-size airplane, and the lawn in front serves as the taxiway.

What's unfolding?
Flick to page 116 to see more!

Going Nowhere

A giant ship apparently stranded in the middle of Hong Kong's Whampoa Garden residential district is actually one of the world's most unusual commercial centers. The size of a real cruise ship, it has four decks with a shopping mall, cinema, restaurants, and even a hotel.

Monster Motorcycle

Roongrojna Sangwongprisarn used recycled materials from old cars and bicycles to create this beast of a bike. The Bangkok-based artist has four studios where he transforms scrapped vehicles into works of art that are exported all over the world. And, unlike most pieces of sculpture, you can actually ride this metal masterpiece.

Think spot!

The average driver spends two weeks of his or her life waiting for traffic lights to change.

29

Mighty Mankind

chapter 2

Paaaniiic!

● What were the greatest dangers about this escape?

Even though it seems fun going through a car wash on top of a car, the dangers were very real. The spinning wheels could have caught any part of me and ripped me apart. The most painful part was the hot wax. It really is hot! I sure was shiny when I finished the car-wash escape!

● How did you overcome the dangers?

I had to try and keep my hands, arms, and legs free of any moving parts and make sure the handcuffs or any of the chains or locks didn't get caught on the spinning wheels. It was impossible to practice going through a car wash so I had to watch the cars go through and get a true sense of timing of how long I would need to escape.

● What was going through your mind when you were going through the car wash?

I was going through each step in my mind of when I needed to escape. It was very important not to be afraid or lose focus, especially when I got hot waxed. Fear will always prevent you from accomplishing your goals and dreams.

Clean Escape

As a Halloween tribute to his hero Harry Houdini, Dean Gunnarson lay spread-eagled, chained, and handcuffed on top of an SUV as it went through an automated car wash. After being whipped by brushes, sprayed with soap, and coated with wax, the shiny Canadian escapologist wriggled free just before the huge blow-dryers got started.

Wheel of Terror

Two children had a lucky escape when a light plane flew into a Ferris wheel they were riding and became lodged between two cabins. Amber Arndell and her brother Jesse were trapped for 90 minutes but escaped unharmed, as did the pilot and his son-in-law. Pilot Paul Cox was trying to land at an airport near Taree, Australia.

Think spot!

John Goldfinch was fishing in Devon, England, when he felt a huge bite. His excitement turned to embarrassment when he reeled in a scuba diver!

Pilot and passenger on board!

Amber and Jesse!

Heart-Stopping Moment

A three-year-old boy was saved by an air-conditioning unit after falling from the eighth-floor balcony of an apartment block in Beijing, China. Neighbors heard him screaming and called the police, but when they noticed he was starting to slip, they launched a daring rescue and pulled him to safety.

Body Work

Feeling Chilly

Winter temperatures often fall below freezing in the northern Chinese province of Hebei, but even during the warm summer months this elderly lady stays at home, huddling under piles of quilts. For the past 13 years she has suffered from a mysterious illness that makes her constantly feel cold.

Folding Face

Tang Shuquan from Chengdu City, China, has offered $15,000 to anyone able to make a face uglier than his. The 43-year-old, who looks perfectly normal when he's not contorting his super-elastic features, can stick out his jaw so far he can even bite his own nose. Would anyone really want to take him on in a face-off?

In a Twist

Xiao Mu, a 26-year-old man from Jiangxi Province, eastern China, demonstrates his flexibility by swiveling his arm up to 360 degrees while balancing cups on the back of his hands, as shown here. People who are very flexible are often said to be double-jointed, but what this really means is that their joints, ligaments, and tendons are just able to stretch farther than the average person's.

RIPLEY RECORDS

▶ **TALLEST MAN EVER** American Robert Wadlow, died 1940—8 feet 11.1 inches.

▶ **TALLEST WOMAN EVER** Zeng Jinlian from China, died 1982—8 feet 1.75 inches.

▶ **TALLEST MAN LIVING** Sultan Kösen from Turkey—8 feet 3 inches.

▶ **TALLEST WOMAN LIVING** Sun Fang from China—7 feet 3 inches.

▶ **SHORTEST MAN ALIVE** Chandra Bahadur Dangi from Nepal—1 foot 9.5 inches.

▶ **SHORTEST WOMAN ALIVE** Jyoti Amge from India—2 feet 0.7 inches.

▶ **TALLEST NATION** The average height of the Dutch is 5 feet 11.2 inches.

▶ **SHORTEST NATION** Cambodians average 5 feet 3.1 inches.

Flexible Physique

Chinese acrobats are well known for dazzling audiences around the world. This respected art has been practiced in China for more than 2,000 years and youngsters begin training at four or five years old. This contortionist is performing in Guangzhou, a southern Chinese city famous for its acrobatic troupes.

Hungry Games

Fast Food

One person's phobia is another's crunchy snack. The Cambodian town of Skuon is famous for its fried tarantulas, which are bred in holes in the ground in nearby villages. They are said to be crispy on the outside and gooey on the inside. The eight-legged delicacy is a popular roadside snack for travelers passing through the town.

Reptile Remedy

If you're looking for a cure for asthma, want to improve your immune system, or need a tonic for your eyesight, a dried lizard might be the answer. Preparation is simple according to specialists in Chinese medicine—you just soak the lizard in water and drink the liquid, although even they admit that it tastes disgusting.

Fits the Bill

While many people are not even aware that ducks have tongues, in Hong Kong they are a popular dish, often served with celery. If you are ever tempted to give them a try, beware—the tongue has a bone running down the middle.

Think spot!

A machine dispensing free desserts for adults uses facial recognition to tell a person's age. If it detects a child, the machine stops.

Candy Craft

Georges Larnicol, who owns a chain of chocolate shops in western France, took to the water in an 11½-foot boat made from chocolate and sugar. The boat, which was powered by an electric motor, took more than 400 hours to make and stayed afloat for 1½ hours. Now Georges has plans for a 40-foot yacht with chocolate masts.

BATEAU CHOCOLAT

What's unfolding?

Flick to page 76 to see more!

PROOF OF EVIDENCE

RUNNING BLIND

Despite being blind since the age of 18, Simon Wheatcroft takes part in some of the world's toughest runs. The British runner originally trained with guides, but now he uses technology to stay on track. A smartphone app provides feedback about his pace and distance that, combined with clues such as gradient or ridges in the path, tell him where he is on his regular route. He was also chosen to carry the Olympic torch for the London 2012 Olympic Games, which he did completely unassisted.

LENGTHY LOBES

Jian Tianjin, a 73-year-old farmer who lives in northeast Taiwan, has earlobes that stretch to his shoulders. His long lobes measure 6½ inches, and are so flexible he can wrap them around his chin.

TWIN TOWN

Luke Foreman, himself a twin, discovered that there were 16 sets of twins among the 380 students in his grade, or 8.42 percent of the class, at his school, Staples High in Westport, Connecticut. The national twin population is only 2 percent.

STOMACH BUGS

Louis Cole could never be called a picky eater. The youth worker, from London, England, has been filmed eating live locusts, wriggling mealworms, a tarantula, and a scorpion, as well as a rotting frog and raw animal eyeballs. The freaky food fan says that most insects taste all right, but he draws the line at cockroaches, which he describes as "vile."

SPIDER MAN

Kevin Jorgeson combines danger and difficulty by clawing his way over boulders up to 45 feet high with holds as narrow as a credit card. The American daredevil, who started rock climbing at the age of 12, can lift his entire body weight with just three fingertips.

FANTASTIC FINGERNAILS

Singer Chris Walton, known as "The Duchess," stopped cutting her fingernails 19 years ago, and they have now reached a combined length of 20 feet. They curl in all directions, yet she can still carry out everyday tasks, use a computer, and play the piano.

EXCESS DIGITS

Akshat Saxena was born with 34 fingers and toes, but no thumbs. The boy from Uttar Pradesh, India, had ten toes on each foot and seven fingers on each hand. He has since had a successful operation to remove some of his extra digits and two of his fingers have been turned into thumbs.

GALLIC TWANG

After a bad bout of flu, British teaching assistant Debie Royston suffered a series of seizures and was unable to speak. Her voice came back after a month, but she had developed a French accent, despite never having visited that country. She was diagnosed with Foreign Accent Syndrome, which occasionally occurs following damage to the brain.

POWERS OF ATTRACTION

Seven-year-old Ivan Stoiljkovic from Croatia is able to stick metal objects, including cutlery, coins, and even heavy pans, to his body. In addition to his magnetic powers, Ivan can lift cement bags weighing 50 pounds.

MATURE MOUNTAINEER

At an age when most people are starting to take it easy, Tamae Watanabe has climbed Mount Everest for the second time. The 73-year-old from Japan originally became the oldest woman to stand on the peak at the age of 63.

One in a Million

THE MISSOURI GIANTESS

Ella Ewing, born in Missouri in 1872, was a small, frail child until the age of nine, when she started to tower over other children. By 22, her mother said she had reached a height of 8 feet 4 inches, although this is unconfirmed, and wore custom-made size 24 shoes. She used her height to earn a good living as a sideshow attraction.

WEIRD

SHORT OF A FULL DECK

Victor Benish Jr. from Detroit, Michigan, had birthmarks on each wrist, one shaped like a spade and the other like a heart. Victor, pictured here in 1932, was a prize-winner in a national Ripley's Believe It or Not! contest.

THAT'S AMAZING

Robert Jones of Pine Bluff, Arkansas, is shown here demonstrating his famous stunt—a thumbstand while balancing on two juggling clubs. For his 50th birthday, Robert cut his cake with one hand while performing a one-handed handstand on the table with the other.

When Norman Falkner of Saskatoon, Canada, had his right leg amputated during World War I, everyone assumed his skating days were over. Norman had other ideas, though, and after many tumbles, he learned that by bending his knee and throwing his body weight from side to side, he was able to propel himself forward. He later performed all over North America.

AWESOME ACHIEVEMENT

HAIRY TEEN

In the past, bearded girls and ladies were the object of great curiosity. During the 19th and early 20th centuries, they often found jobs in circus sideshows. In many cases, the excess hair is caused by a condition called hypertrichosis.

HUMAN MARVEL

Sideshow performer Francesco Lentini was born in Sicily in 1889 with three legs, four feet, and 16 toes. His legs were also all different lengths. However, he learned to run, ride a bicycle, and even ice-skate.

FANCY FOOTWORK

This double-footed horse belonging to R. van Wert of Cincinnati, Ohio, was photographed in 1930. You wouldn't want that hoof standing on your foot!

WOW!

41

Gene Genius

Full House

Ziona Chana, who once married ten women in a year, is head of an enormous family. His 100-room, four-story mansion in Baktwang, India, houses Ziona and his 39 wives, 94 children, 14 daughters-in-law, and 33 grandchildren— a total of 181 people. A typical family meal might consist of 30 chickens, 132 pounds of potatoes, and 220 pounds of rice.

Bungay vs. Bungay

The town of Bungay in eastern England hosted a soccer match in which all the players, officials, and reserves were named Bungay. With just 455 people named Bungay in Britain, the soccer club had to recruit players from as far away as the US and Australia. Carla Bungay was the mascot and Dr. Elizabeth Bungay was on hand to treat injuries.

Extended Family

It is rare to find five generations of a family alive at the same time, but this photograph, taken in 1939, shows eight generations of a family of Cree Indians, a tribe of Native Americans who lived in the US and Canada. The youngest member of the family is the great-great-great-great-great-grandchild of the oldest.

Light Locks

The inhabitants of the Solomon Islands, east of Papua New Guinea, have puzzled scientists for decades—they are very dark skinned but five to ten percent of them have bright blond hair. Until recently, scientists thought the blond hair came from Europeans who had paired with islanders, but now they believe the flaxen hair comes from a single gene specific only to the islanders—and it's a different gene from the one that causes blondness in northern Europe.

Unordinary People

A Bigger Splash

Every September, more than 25,000 avid swimmers, ranging in age from ten to over 80, gather at Taiwan's largest lake for a two-mile race called the Swimming Carnival of Sun Moon Lake. Unlike most competitions, participants are asked to swim across the lake in a slow, relaxed style so they can appreciate the crystal clear waters and beautiful mountain scenery. Some groups even treat the mass swim as a social event, pulling floating picnic baskets behind them and chatting as they go.

Extreme Mechanic

When Emile Leray's car broke down in the Sahara Desert, he had enough food and water to last ten days. With little chance of rescue, the French mechanic decided his only chance of survival was to build a motorcycle from the parts of his Citroen 2CV. Twelve days later, with just a pint of water left, he drove the makeshift bike back to civilization.

Pint-Sized Rodeo

Called the toughest sport on wool, mutton busting is a chance for young broncos to get an early taste of Wild West adventure. Wearing protective vests, children under the age of six cling to the backs of sheep, and whoever stays on their wooly steed longest wins.

Think spot!

Tujia people from China have a tradition of "weeping marriage." Brides start to cry a month before the wedding, then friends join in.

MAXIMIZE

Mind Over Matter

The Shaolin Wu-Shu Warriors wowed audiences when the Chinese State Circus appeared at Scotland's Edinburgh Festival. Shaolin martial arts are taught by monks of the Shaolin Temple, in Henan Province, northeastern China, and include meditation and breathing techniques to increase reaction speeds and block out pain. Performer Song Atmin is pictured here as a fellow warrior uses a sledgehammer to smash four bricks balanced on his head.

High Expectations

Nerves of Steel

This worker sweeping the Aizhai suspension bridge would see the spectacular sight of Dehang Canyon if he stopped to admire the view. The bridge in China's Hunan Province is 1,102 feet high and has an amazing span of 3,858 feet. It is part of an expressway linking Chongqing municipality and Changsha city, which shortens the journey time from a few days to eight hours.

Head for Heights

An extraordinary craze has seen hundreds of young Russian thrill seekers scaling Moscow's highest structures without safety harnesses. This climber is relaxing on the arm of Peter the Great, the eighth-tallest statue in the world, measuring a terrifying 322 feet high.

Cable Guy

Fearless free-climber Stephan Siegrist edged his way along a 11,453-foot cable-car wire while hanging upside down from pickaxes 82 feet above the ground. The Swiss daredevil is one of five climbers who compete professionally for the Mammut Pro Team. Each team member took on a unique challenge in an unusual location, including an elevator shaft and a scrap metal yard.

Think spot! In May 2011, Jed Mildon pulled off the world's first triple backflip on a BMX in his hometown of Taupo, New Zealand.

Ice Warrior

Mark Sollors took full advantage of the stunning glacial terrain in Methven on New Zealand's South Island. The intrepid Finnish snowboarder hit the top of this natural quarter-pipe, looking down at the 40-foot drop just inches in front of him.

Man's Best Friends

Monkey House

Monkey lover Connie Tibbs, who runs a pet shop on the family farm in Pekin, Illinois, is mom to five snow macaques as well as her three teenage children. The monkeys live in the house, wear diapers, take baths in the family tub, and accompany Connie wherever she goes. One even shares her bed, dressed in its own pajamas. They are part of a large menagerie, including camels, horses, potbellied pigs, dogs, cats, rabbits, degus (small rodents), miniature donkeys, and a serval (an African wildcat).

● In what ways have you had to alter your home and your life to accommodate the monkeys?
I've had to set up spaces for them where they can't get into any trouble or get hurt when I'm not around to watch them.

● What do people say to you when you're out with them?
Everyone always thinks they are so cute. They are always surprised to see me walk in with a monkey on my head!

● Are the monkeys affectionate?
For the most part they are very loving and wanting to give kisses. They can get upset when something scares them, though.

● Monkeys or husband. Which comes first?
MONKEYS! My monkeys are like my kids. I always have their needs first.

Take the Plunge

The "Bulls to the Sea" Festival takes place each July in Denia, Spain. A young bull is let loose in an arena that is open to the harbor on one side. Men and boys tease the bull and are forced to jump into the sea when it chases them. Occasionally, the bull ends up in the water, too, and is towed back to shore by boat.

Think spot!

Alfred David regularly walks around Brussels, Belgium, in a penguin costume, and wants to be buried near Antarctica in a penguin-adorned coffin.

Breakfast Time!

If you stay at Giraffe Manor, don't be surprised if you end up sharing your breakfast with a very long-necked creature. The hotel in Nairobi, Kenya, provides guests with an unusual vacation—giraffes share their rooms and breakfast table! The 140-acre estate is also home to one of the world's rarest breeds of giraffe, the Rothschild.

What's unfolding? Flick to page 125 to see more!

Wild Life

chapter 3

Behaving Like Animals

Pick Your Own

Goats in Morocco love the berries of the argan tree, and it is not unusual to see as many as 16 of them balancing on branches up to 30 feet high as they seek out the fruits. The goats digest the fruit's flesh, but not the nuts, which are made into a highly prized oil, used in cooking and cosmetics.

Bird's-Eye View

Aerial wildlife photographer Bobby Haas from Dallas, Texas, was taking shots of a shifting flock of flamingos in the Mexican province of Yucatán when the birds spontaneously gathered into a giant flamingo-shaped formation. He just managed to capture this fleeting, once-in-a-lifetime image before the birds dispersed.

Resourceful Rodent

Charlie the chipmunk wanted a cool drink of orange juice but, as many people have discovered, it's no use sucking on a bent straw. Charlie soon found the solution—he bypassed the straw and dove headfirst into the glass.

What a Hoot!

Two tiny, burrowing owlets made themselves at home in wildlife-park keeper Jimmy Robinson's apartment after being hatched in an incubator at a local hawk conservancy. The pair, named Linford and Christie, huddled in all kinds of weird nooks and crannies, including cups, bookcases, and Jimmy's dog basket.

Hey, Good-Looking!

Cyclops of the Sea

Mexican fisherman Enrique Lucero León discovered this rare baby cyclops shark by accident. He found the one-eyed, albino fetus, along with its nine normal siblings, when he cut open a pregnant dusky shark he had caught in the Gulf of California in Mexico.

Eye see you!

Mature Mustache

Alfie, a thirteen-year-old Shire-cross stallion from Gloucestershire, England, is clearly proud of his unusual facial hair. The seven-inch, curly, golden mustache sprouted from his lip when he reached maturity, and all efforts to clip it have been in vain. Just the sight of the scissors makes Alfie bolt across the stable to avoid the snip.

Think spot!

Toby, a Jack Russell terrier, got his just desserts when he chewed up his owner's mail. The mix of adhesive and wet paper temporarily glued his mouth shut.

A pink bottlenose dolphin, spotted in Calcasieu Lake, Louisiana, could be the only one of its kind. Charter boat captain Erik Rue photographed the animal when it surfaced in the inland saltwater estuary, north of the Gulf of Mexico. While the unique creature looks pink, its reddish eyes prove that it is actually an albino.

Creature Features

When Tony Doust spotted this bulging tree trunk at Bedgebury National Pinetum in Kent, England, he realized it looked uncannily like the face of a hippopotamus. This isn't the first time Tony has come across a tree masquerading as an animal. He found a lookalike of cartoon bird Woody Woodpecker at Scotney Castle, also in Kent.

Plucky and Lucky

Saved by a Whisker

When a driver in Rio Verde, Brazil, felt his car losing power, he was shocked to find a kitten's head sticking out of the exhaust. He assumed the animal was dead and drove to his local garage, but when they started to take the engine apart, they discovered the kitten was still alive. They rushed the engine and the kitten to the local fire station, where firefighters cut the lucky creature free. After abdominal surgery, the kitten was put up for adoption.

Prickly Situation

A young bulldog learned a sharp lesson when she had a run-in with a porcupine near her home in Norman, Oklahoma. It took a veterinarian and two nurses two hours to pluck more than 500 quills from Bella Mae's face and feet after her encounter with the spiky critter. She recovered completely.

RIPLEY RECORDS

▶ **LONGEST JOURNEY HOME** After walking 2,000 miles across Australia, Jimpa, a Labrador-boxer cross, arrived back at his old home in Pimpinio, Australia.

▶ **LONGEST SURF RIDE BY A DOG** Abbie Girl, a kelpie (an Australian sheepdog), surfed a wave 351 feet 8 inches long at Ocean Beach Dog Beach, California.

▶ **LONGEST JUMP BY A KANGAROO** In January 1951, while being chased, a female red kangaroo leapt a distance of 42 feet in one bound.

▶ **LONGEST TIME IN A BATHROOM CAVITY WALL** A cat spent four days in a wall after builders accidentally sealed it in while decorating a bathroom in Clausthal-Zellerfeld, Germany. Firefighters had to smash up the new bathroom to release it!

Do you come here often?

Balancing Act

Two young goats found themselves in a tight spot after wandering onto the narrow ledge of a remote 60-foot-high railway bridge in Helena, Montana. The creatures' plight was discovered when a passing motorist alerted a local charity. They enlisted the help of a nearby coal-mining company, which used a crane to pluck the animals to safety.

MAXIMIZE

Web Blanket

When floodwaters forced thousands of residents to evacuate their homes in Wagga Wagga, Australia, the local wolf spiders made sure they were high and dry. These ground-dwelling spiders have a natural instinct to escape rising waters by climbing blades of grass and spinning long threads of silk that get caught by the wind and carry the spiders to another location. Millions of these silk streamers formed a blanket that covered vast areas of the city.

Shrubs were completely cocooned in sticky webs.

How Do I Look?

King of Bugs

Amateur photographer Winston Jansen was surprised to see a familiar face when he came across this stinkbug on an expedition in the forests of Singapore. The jet-black hairstyle, dark eyes, and distinctive sideburns bore a remarkable resemblance to rock 'n' roll legend Elvis Presley.

Duck Diaper

Barbershop owner Mrs. Deng, from Guiyang in China's Guizhou Province, was tired of cleaning up after her pet duck, so she came up with the idea of using a shoe cover as a diaper. Now the duck has become a local celebrity and has free run of the shop.

Dogs in Disguise

The latest craze in China is to paint dogs to resemble other animals. Chow Chow dogs have their golden fur dyed black and white to look like pandas, and retrievers are transformed into tigers.

Think spot!

A tiny frog that glides from tree to tree in the Borneo rain forest has bright green skin at night and turns brown during the day. Its eyes change color, too.

Good Hair Day

This Mary River turtle's green Mohawk is actually algae, which usually coats the turtle's shell. The strange-looking reptile has long, powerful limbs with large, webbed feet and an outsized, hooked tail, which absorbs oxygen so it can stay underwater for long periods. It is only found in the Mary River, and is one of the most endangered turtles in eastern Australia.

What's unfolding?

Flick to page 20 to see more!

Help Is at Hand

Canine Carrier

If dogs in the US and UK keep piling on the pounds, more than half will be severely overweight by 2022, so a British pet insurance company has created a prototype stair lift for plump pooches. The machine features a special "paw push" start button close enough to the ground for the animal to reach with an outstretched leg.

Feline Houdini

Ksyusha the Himalayan kitten likes to squeeze herself into tight spaces, but even her owner Yuriy Korotun from Moscow, Russia, was surprised to find her inside this glass jar. The mischievous escape artist, nicknamed "Mewdini," has freed herself easily so far, but when she grows up she may need to look for a larger jar.

Tablet Cure

Maia the hen stopped laying eggs after a fox ate her companion, so her owner Ashley Wood from England tried showing her films of chickens on his iPad. After the virtual encouragement, she went back to producing five eggs a week.

Think spot!

In northern Norway the sun does not rise in midwinter, so to reduce the number of accidents, 2,000 reindeer have been fitted with reflective collars and antler tags.

Gotcha!

Gentle Giant

Keepers at Pocatello Zoo, Idaho, were concerned when Shooter the elk tried to dip his hooves into his water tank, then dunked his head in the water. To their amazement, when Shooter raised his head he had a tiny marmot between his jaws. The massive elk put the rodent on the ground and gently nudged it with his foot until it ran off into the bushes.

Stand Out in a Crowd

Flipped Features

Herbert the turbot swims in the opposite direction of his fellow flatfish at a British sea life center, because his eyes are on the wrong side of his head. Normally a turbot's right eye moves around so it is next to the left, meaning they swim on their right side, but Herbert's have moved the opposite way, so he swims on his left.

Think spot!

After losing 200 sheep to rustlers, a British farmer dyed his flock bright orange to deter thieves.

Monster Croc

A saltwater crocodile measuring 20 feet 3 inches long and weighing more than a ton was captured alive in Bunawan, a remote town in the Philippines, in 2011, following a three-week hunt. The giant croc, named Lolong, was suspected of killing two people and attacking more. It was hauled from a creek by about 100 people, but sadly died at the new ecotourism park in 2013.

Superstar Sheep

Shrek the sheep became a celebrity in New Zealand after going on the run for six years to avoid the shearers. By the time he was captured, his massive fleece weighed 60 pounds—about six times more than average. After a career that included TV shows, national tours, and meeting the prime minister, Shrek lived to the age of 15, making him one of the world's oldest sheep, as well as the wooliest.

AFTER

STRIKE A NOTE

Shrek's giant fleece would provide enough yarn for:

✳ 20 suits

✳ 120 five-foot scarves

✳ 65 loose-knit sweaters

✳ 500 pairs of socks

✳ 410 pairs of gloves

✳ 280 beanie hats

Phew, I'm hot!

BEFORE

PROOF OF EVIDENCE

... Love you

STRANGE SOUL MATE

A mute swan named Schwani has fallen in love with a tractor, according to hotel owner Hermann-Josef Hericks. The swan, from Velen in northwest Germany, rushes over as soon as the engine starts up and follows the tractor everywhere. Swans are said to mate for life, but Schwani also has eyes for an excavator on the building site next door.

BED CRASHER DUMMIES

Thousands of people share their beds with their pets, so a furniture store has produced "crash test dummy" dogs and cats in different sizes. Now bed buyers can check if the mattress will be big enough for them and their animal companions.

DOGGY SUNSCREEN

Human sunscreen can be toxic for dogs if they lick it off, so a company has launched a sun protection line specially formulated for dogs!

BLESS YOU!

The Burmese snub-nosed monkey is a rare species of Colobine monkey found in northern Burma (Myanmar). The monkeys' noses are so upturned that the animals sneeze when it rains. To avoid getting water up their noses, they sit with their heads between their knees on rainy days.

BEAR-FACED CHEEK

A mother bear and her two cubs took a dip in a swimming pool in California to escape the heat. After ten minutes, the bears ambled back to the woods, just before animal control officers arrived.

EARTHQUAKE UNEARTHS CAT

Three years after going missing, Fritz the cat turned up at Melbourne's Lost Dogs Home after an earthquake shook the Australian city. Thanks to his microchip, he was reunited with his owner, Laura Kapadia.

IN A SPIN

An eight-week-old kitten named Princess had a miraculous escape after climbing into the washing machine when her owner, Susan Gordon of Aberdeen, Scotland, wasn't looking. Princess was trapped in the machine for an hour while it completed its washing cycle. Luckily, she survived with nothing worse than bruising and sore eyes.

TRUE LOVE

When a pregnant orangutan was quarantined at China's Yunnan Wild Animal Park, her mate missed her so much he tried to dig a tunnel to her.

HIPPO HYGIENIST

A four-foot-wide mouth needs special oral care, so keepers at the Shanghai Zoo clean the teeth of their hippos using a giant toothbrush. Wild hippos eat grass, but at the zoo they eat fruit and vegetables, which stick in their teeth.

Help!

SURROGATE MOM

Staff at China's Wuhan Zoo were having problems caring for an orphaned zebra until they noticed he became excited when he saw keeper Chen Nong wearing a black-and-white-striped T-shirt. Nong took on the job of feeding the zebra, but the baby would only take milk from him when he was wearing the striped shirt.

CURIOUS KITTEN

A kitten squeezed through a hole in the bathroom and fell 15 feet through the inner wall to the ground floor. Twelve hours later, her owner heard the kitten's cries and an animal rescue specialist cut through the wall, releasing the kitten unharmed.

Too Clever by Far

Equine Aquatics

For the past twenty years, Lightning the Wonder Horse has entertained audiences at the Magic Forest amusement park in Lake George, New York, by diving ten feet into a large pool of water. After completing his dive, Lightning climbs up a ramp to the applause of his fans, and is rewarded with a large bucket of oats.

Think spot!

A whale shark found an easy way to vacuum up the huge amount of small fish it needs to eat each day. The 26-foot giant was spotted sucking fish from a trawler's net.

Who's a Clever Boy?

A pet budgie escaped from its owner's home in Yokohama, Japan, and found its way into a city hotel. It was taken to a police station and suddenly recited its home address and its name, repeating, "You're pretty, Piko-chan." The bird was soon reunited with its owner, Fumie Takahashi.

Tweeting Cats

Owners who wonder what their cat gets up to when they're away could stay in touch by following their pet on Twitter. Kitty Twitty was invented by American product developer Marc de Vinck. When the cat swats a hovering bird on a wire, the gadget posts the news. He suggests that a sensor could be attached to a food bowl and cat flap, too.

INTERVIEW

Peter, how did you spot Sammy?
I live by the River Dart in the village of Dittisham, near Dartmouth, England. At about 7:30 one evening, I looked across the garden toward the river and saw the bow of an orange rubber dinghy pointing up in the air, and a large black creature trying to haul itself aboard. When I woke before five the next morning, Sammy was still in the orange dinghy, fast asleep. So I ran down to our slipway, jumped into my own dinghy, and went out to take a closer look. He was big and overhung both ends of his little dinghy, which he lay in like a hammock, his head resting in the bow and his flippers over the stern.

So Sammy was on vacation?
He stayed for the next two weeks, spending most of the time snoozing in his dinghy and occasionally sliding back into the river to go fishing. People even came to visit him, until one day he left. We were surprised he stayed as long as did, with limited seal food choices, but hope he'll come to stay again one day.

Relaxing on the River

Seals are often seen basking on rocks, but gray seal Sammy enjoyed soaking up the sun in his very own leisure craft. Sammy visited the River Dart in Dittisham, England, where he launched himself onto a dinghy as if it were a chaise lounge.

Baby, I Was Born This Way

Carrottop

This bright orange baby monkey really stood out from the crowd at London Zoo, England. The rare Francois' langur monkey bears no resemblance to its black-haired parents, but its fur will begin to darken when it is three months old. Experts think the orange color is designed to attract other females to help out with the baby-sitting.

Meeow

Meeow

Double Take

A rag-doll cat born with two mouths, two noses, and three eyes was never expected to survive, but to everyone's surprise the two-faced cat has celebrated his 12th birthday. Frankenlouie, who lives with his owner, Marty Stevens, in Worcester, Massachusetts, can see out of only two of his eyes and can eat with only one of his mouths, but both his noses work.

Mind My Tail

Calves' tails are normally between five and eight inches long, but a calf born on Jennifer Showalter's farm in Fairfield, Virginia, had a tail that was an extraordinary five feet long. At that length, it is bound to get trampled on by the rest of the herd, and so it has been trimmed for safety.

Think spot!

Giant pandas mark their territory by performing a handstand and urinating as high as possible up the side of a tree.

Master of Disguise

The leaf-tailed gecko's clever camouflage helps it blend into its natural environment in the rain forests of Madagascar. Its body is usually mottled brown, but it can adapt its skin color to match its surroundings, turning green, yellow, or orange. This makes the lizard pretty tricky for predators to spot.

I'm here!

Science Class

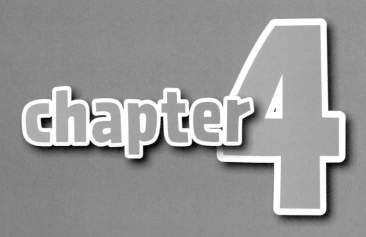

chapter 4

Going Digital

AFTER

Good-Bye DIY

Change your decor from pink playroom to indoor jungle at the click of a mouse. The amazing transformations are created using two projectors that beam colors, textures, and patterns into every corner of the room. The Mr. Beam light projector was developed by a Dutch team, who built a completely white living room to use as a canvas.

Think spot!

Neal and Maddie Love bought a town on eBay for $360,000. The town of Wauconda, Washington, has its own zip code, store, gas pump, post office, and house.

BEFORE

Big Head

Taras Lesko from Covington, Washington, made this 3-D, scale model of his own head entirely from paper. After photographing his head from all angles, Taras used computer softwear to design the model. He then printed it out in pieces, before assembling them to create the giant head.

Literal Laptop

Dutch inventors Erik de Nijs and Tim Smit have designed a pair of jeans with a built-in computer keyboard, mouse, and speakers. Wireless technology connects the jeans to the computer and allows the user to move around while typing. If they make it onto the market, they are expected to retail for around $400.

Modern Renaissance

Photoshop wizards used their skills to send screen idols, including Angelina Jolie, Brad Pitt, and Hugh Laurie, back in time. The winning portrait gallery of Renaissance superstars was picked from entries in a competition to create convincing copies of the Old Masters featuring modern celebrities, organized by Worth1000.

Growth Patterns

Microbial Masterpiece

Zachary Copfer creates images in petri dishes using glowing bacteria. A photographic negative is laid on top of the bacteria and exposed to radiation to produce sterilized patches that become dark spots. The microbiologist-turned-artist uses the technique, called "bacteriography," to create portraits of famous artists and scientists, underlining the fusion of art and science in his work.

" When science and art are brought together, unbelievable things can happen. I combined my past experience with bacteria, as a microbiologist, and newfound knowledge of photography. The result was a process I named bacteriography. Using a petri dish full of bacteria, a special photographic negative, and ultraviolet radiation (like that from the Sun), I can grow a photograph in living bacteria. **"**

Festering Foodscapes

Inspired by a pot of long-forgotten boiled potatoes, Heikki Leis has produced a series of images called "Afterlife" using moldy vegetables that resemble alien landscapes. The Estonian artist's favorite subjects are beet, potato, turnip, corn, and pumpkin, but he admits that these are also the smelliest, requiring a strong stomach to get as close as he does.

Think Spot!

There are more than 70 species of mushrooms that glow in the dark. Some are so bright that you could use them to read in a dark room.

Hiccup.

Cocktail Dress

Scientists from the University of Western Australia have created a fabric by adding bacteria to wine. Acetobacter turns wine or other alcoholic drinks into vinegar, leaving a rubbery, skinlike layer on the top. This layer is collected and modeled on an inflatable mannequin to form a dress. When the mannequin is deflated, the garment remains.

Call 911!

Dental Detector

Scientists at Princeton University have developed a wireless sensor made of graphene—a layer of carbon just one-atom thick—that can be stuck to a tooth to monitor a patient's health. The sensor is able to detect very small amounts of bacteria and certain viruses, to give an early warning of disease and infection.

Brain Food

Even the most die-hard chocoholic might think twice before taking a bite out of a chocolate brain, but Andy Millns happily chowed down on a replica of his own gray matter. The British IT expert used a 3-D printer to create a mini-model of his brain using a computer map based on an MRI scan, then he made a latex mold and filled it with liquid chocolate.

Mystery Condition

These pictures show the same woman, but they were taken just five years apart. Nguyen Thi Phuong from Vietnam appeared to age five decades in a matter of days following an allergic reaction to seafood. Doctors have since uncovered the rare condition, only the second case of its kind diagnosed, and after a month of treatment, her skin has improved.

BEFORE

Think spot!

Tears turned to cheers when a 28-year-old man was found to be alive just before his funeral near Luxor, Egypt. He was declared dead after suffering a heart attack.

Watch This Space

Mystery Marbles

Steve Hornsby from Bournemouth, England, found his lawn scattered with blue, marble-sized balls after a sudden hailstorm. A scientist at his local university suggested that the transparent, jellylike spheres could be invertebrate eggs from the sea, while others thought they might be globules of a substance used in diapers.

RIPLEY RECORDS

▶ **LONGEST SPACE FLIGHT** Valeri Polyakov stayed at the Mir space station for 437.7 days, during which time he orbited the Earth about 7,075 times and traveled 186,887,000 miles before returning to Earth on March 22, 1995.

▶ **FARTHEST FROM EARTH** The *Apollo 13* crew, while passing over the far side of the moon on April 15, 1970, were 248,655 miles from Earth.

▶ **FIRST WEDDING IN SPACE** US couple Erin Finnegan and Noah Fulmor became the first couple to have a weightless wedding on June 20, 2009. During the ceremony on G-Force One, the bride, groom, and their guests experienced zero gravity for fifteen 30-second periods.

▶ **FIRST FAMILY ON THE MOON** Moonwalker Charles Duke left a portrait of his family on the lunar surface in 1972.

Strange Encounter

In 1973, Jeff Greenhaw, chief of police in Falkville, Alabama, received a call claiming that a UFO had landed just outside the town. The chief drove to the location and came face-to-face with a humanoid figure wearing a silvery, metallic suit. He picked up his camera and shot four Polaroids before the creature fled, never to be seen again.

Transporter Pod

Researchers from Queen's University, Canada, have created a video conferencing system that allows people to talk as if they were in the same room. Each person stands in front of an acrylic cylinder while a 3-D camera captures his or her image, which is projected inside a cylinder at the other end. You can even walk around it and see the person's back and sides.

Think spot!

Limited-edition space rings are made of gold that was sent into space in a suborbital research rocket. They retail at an astronomical $17,000 a pair.

Reminder of Home

In 2010, Dawn Melville from Cumbria, England, was on vacation in Kissimmee, Florida, while ash from an Icelandic volcano was disrupting flights over Europe. She and her husband were wondering whether they would make it home when they spotted this cloud in the shape of Great Britain—a reminder of home!

MAXIMIZE

Micro-Cosmos

After shooting 360° panoramic photographs as a hobby, Alexandre Duret-Lutz had the idea of stitching the images together to form what he calls "wee planets." The computer scientist, who lives near Paris, France, chooses a starting point and takes pictures of the horizon and the sky in every direction. Then he assembles up to 100 pictures side by side on a computer and uses stereographic projection to form them into a sphere. His mini-worlds might feature a small forest, a cityscape, or a solitary landmark.

Street Life

Party Trick

Fans of glow sticks can go one better with these glow-in-the-dark jeans. The glow, which is recharged by natural or artificial light, comes from a phosphorescent coating applied to the denim. During the day, they look like standard jeans, but after dark they start to shine. Perfect for party people who want to stand out—or cyclists who like to be seen.

Think Spot!

A cell phone company has filed a patent for a magnetic tattoo that will vibrate to alert smartphone users to incoming calls.

Moshi-Moshi

You may be tempted to order takeout if you choose an iPhone case from Japanese company iMeshi. Their cell phone covers are adorned with realistic Japanese specialties, from sushi to ramen noodles. If your tastes are more Western than Asian, the bacon-and-egg phone cover would be just right for breakfast meetings.

Smart Car

The Fun-Vii, unveiled in Tokyo, Japan, is a concept car that thinks it's a smartphone. The futuristic, interactive car can be used as a display space, and both exterior and interior designs can be changed as easily as downloading an app. The car is designed to interface with smartphones and other road users, adding social and safety elements to the driving experience.

Hello! Mr. J. Smith

BEFORE

Flatpack Boat

If you're planning a trip to the lake, why not take a boat with you? The Foldboat packs into a 60 x 31 inch parcel and is made from a sheet of plastic. It comes with inflatable cushions that double up as flotation devices, plus a pair of oars. The origami boat is the brainchild of students Max Frommeld and Arno Mathies from London's Royal College of Art.

Phew, how much farther?

AFTER

What's unfolding?

Flick to page 139 to see more!

Twin Peak

As sunlight hit the snow-covered slopes of Grimming Mountain in Steiermark, Austria, in October 2012, an incredibly accurate portrait of Albert Einstein's face appeared! The German-born physicist was famous for developing the theory of relativity and forever changing our understanding of the universe, but even he might have struggled to explain the eerie apparition.

Top Prize for Bug Eyes

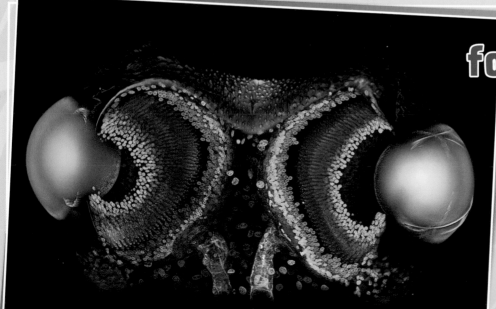

This eye-popping close-up of a daddy longlegs took first prize in the 2010 Olympus BioScapes Digital Imaging Competition. Dr. Igor Siwanowicz captured the wide-eyed arachnid through a light microscope. The picture shows the eyes' lenses (two large ovals), the retinas, and the optic nerves trailing down the center.

Wonder Woman

Meet Dot. At just 0.3 inches tall, she's the world's tiniest action hero and stars in the world's smallest film. The film, simply called *Dot*, was produced for Nokia by Aardman—the creators of Wallace and Gromit. Animators used a 3-D printer to make 50 versions of Dot and then filmed her through a CellScope, a microscope for mobile phones. Dot runs for her life, climbs flowers, and escapes on a bumble bee in the action film.

Life in the Shadows

At first, the heaps of wood, furniture, and metal scraps in the middle of an art gallery floor in London appear to be nothing more than piles of junk. In fact, they have been meticulously arranged by artists Tim Noble and Sue Webster so that when they're lit by a beam of light, at exactly the right angle, they create human-shaped shadows.

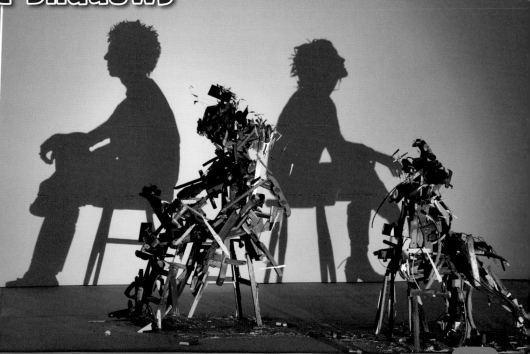

Doctor, Doctor

Shocking Stunt

Illusionist and endurance artist David Blaine completed a death-defying stunt by withstanding one million volts, for three days and three nights. David stood on top of a 20-foot pole absorbing the electrical currents without eating or sleeping. When he tried to drink some water, the electric discharge from a Telsa coil gave him an electric shock, so he didn't try again. He recovered soon after completing the stunt, unharmed.

Think spot!

A genetically engineered virus has been developed that can convert mechanical energy into electricity. In the future a person's heartbeat could power a pacemaker.

I Spy with My Giant Eye

This giant eyeball, measuring around the size of a softball, was found washed up on Pompano Beach, Florida, separated from the body of the sea creature it came from. Experts have agreed it probably belongs to either a large swordfish or a giant squid, although scientists say it most likely comes from a swordfish due to its round iris—a squid's iris is always a W shape.

Outta Space

The Space Shuttle *Endeavour* made a journey unlike any of its others in October 2012. After 25 missions into space—that's nearly a year spent in space—the *Endeavour* made its final 12-mile trip on land, past houses and shopping malls, sometimes only inches away from buildings. The Shuttle, originally housed in LAX Airport, made the two-day journey to the California Science Center, where it is now on display.

Fastenings Phobia

A fear of spiders, snakes, or heights is not uncommon, but Hannah Matthews panics at the sight of a button. The student has been receiving counseling because she is worried that her condition, called koumpounophobia, could affect her performance in job interviews if someone is wearing buttons.

PROOF OF EVIDENCE

Boo!

Happiness Dispenser

As part of their Open Happiness campaign, Coca-Cola installed a vending machine at the National University of Singapore with the words *Hug Me* in place of the company's logo. Students who obey the instruction and give the machine a squeeze get a free can of soda.

SOCIAL PETWORKING

More than half of all pet owners post about their animals on social networks, and one in ten pets has its own profile. Boo, a cute dog on Facebook, is liked by nearly 6½ million people, while Sockington the cat has nearly 1½-million Twitter followers and has tweeted more than 7,000 times!

PEOPLE POWER

A British outdoor gym company makes good use of the energy that exercise enthusiasts expend on their equipment. As users burn off the calories on the free-to-use cross trainer, hand bike, fitness bike, and recumbent bike, their efforts are converted into useable electricity.

SUBWAY SUPERSTORE

Busy commuters in South Korea can shop in a virtual supermarket inside the subway station as they wait for their train. Realistic re-creations of the aisles are displayed on the subway walls, and shoppers scan the goods with their smartphones. The shopping is then delivered to their door when they arrive home.

TECH TOY

Sphero is a color-changing robotic ball that is controlled by a tilt, touch, or swing of a smartphone or tablet. It can be used in races, to follow a path, as a golf ball, or as an expensive cat toy.

Poo!

SPACE SCENT

NASA is trying to re-create the smell of space for training purposes. Astronauts agree that space has a unique odor, which they describe variously as meaty, metallic, and reminiscent of welding fumes.

Cooking Vessel

There's no need to take your catch home if you are the proud owner of a Barbecue Dining Boat. The donut-shaped boat has a built-in grill in the center with seating for ten around the outside. The boat moves at a leisurely 2½ mph, and sells for $50,000.

GAME BOY

Aaron Bond, a 13-year-old British schoolboy, wrote his own smartphone game by watching tutorials online. His friend Sebastian McNeil came up with the idea for Spud Run, which involved navigating a mutant potato through a maze.

VIRAL VIDEO

Five-month-old Emerson from London, Canada, became an Internet sensation after his dramatic reaction to the sound of his mother blowing her nose was posted on YouTube. It attracted more than 21 million viewers during the first four months it was online.

QUIRKY APP

An iPhone app called Blower claims to extinguish birthday candles without any accessories. It uses the built-in speaker and plays sound at sufficient volume to generate a vibration strong enough to blow out the candles.

FLYING FINGERS

in 2011, Eduard Saakashvili, the teenage son of Georgian President Mikheil Saakashvili, typed the English alphabet on an iPad with one hand in just 5.26 seconds—that's 4.94 letters per second. Eduard practiced for months to prepare for the challenge.

Body Conscious

Cyborg Artist

Color-blind artist Neil Harbisson from Northern Ireland, UK, can only see in black and white. Since 2004, however, he has worn an "eyeborg," a device in front of his forehead that detects the light's hue and converts it into a sound frequency. It also translates the saturation of the color into volume, so a vivid red will sound louder than a paler shade of red.

Think spot!

A bolt of lightning can travel at up to 136,000 mph and reach temperatures of 55,000 °F—hotter than the surface of the Sun!

Lung Power

The AIRE mask breathes new life into electronic gadgets. The mask contains tiny wind turbines that convert exhaled air into energy to recharge cell phones and MP3 players. Inventor Joao Paulo Lammoglia from Rio de Janeiro, Brazil, suggests that it can be worn while sleeping, walking, running, or even reading a book.

Bionic Eye

A British man is hoping to see his wife of seven years for the first time thanks to a tiny electronic chip embedded at the back of his eye. Chris James lost his sight more than 20 years ago because of a condition called retinitis pigmentosa, in which light-sensitive cells in the eye stop working. The microchip converts light into electrical impulses that travel to the brain. As a result he can now make out the outline of shapes.

● *Chris, how is your vision progressing?*
As I've only had the implant for a few months, I'm still getting used to it. Shortly after the microchip was switched on, I could see light when I had a flashlight flashed in my eye. I can also detect light-colored shapes on a dark background—for example, a white cup and saucer on a black table.

● *That's amazing! Can you describe it?*
At the moment, it's a bit like looking out of a dirty window. I can pick up on where light is coming from, for instance, a window. As time progresses and I get used to the implant, I may be able to identify objects and my surroundings.

● *Have you had to adjust your life again?*
I'm still using my white cane to get around, especially for my job. Being a clinical experiment, it's not certain exactly what I will be able to see over time. For me, it's a question of my brain trying to make sense of my surroundings and take in images—it's been a while since my brain has had to do this. Once my brain starts to get used to this, then there may be some tasks I can do without assistance.

95

Danger Zone

On a Wing and a Prayer

Stuntman Gary Connery leaped from a helicopter flying at 2,400 feet without using a parachute and made a safe landing in a field in southern England. Wearing a custom-made wingsuit, the British daredevil dropped for three seconds at speeds of up to 80 mph before spreading his wings like a flying squirrel. The death-defying flight lasted for 50 seconds before Gary plowed into a 350-foot-long landing strip made of 18,600 cardboard boxes.

Yeee-haaaa!

Aim for these boxes, Gary!

Water Fall

This is the moment just before experienced surfer Ross Clarke-Jones almost broke his neck and died as a wave the size of a two-story building came crashing down on him. That day, he had jet-skied out to the world's biggest storms that brew off the coast of New Zealand to ride the colossal waves they create. Luckily, Ross survived the near-fatal incident and emergency surgery prevented any lasting damage.

Crack Team

Two British climbers have inched their way up the Century Crack, a 120-foot split in Utah's Canyonlands. Tom Randall and Pete Whittaker forced their limbs into nooks and crannies to climb up what is said to be the most difficult crack in the world. Tom even built a replica of the gap in his cellar so the pair could practice the tricky ascent.

STRIKE A NOTE
Wide Boyz

The "Wide Boyz," as Tom and Pete are known, trained for two years before tackling the Century Crack. Here's how they prepared . . .

※ 17,500 feet of horizontal upside-down climbing

※ 250,000 core and abdominal conditioning movements

※ 42,300 pull-ups and bicep curls

※ almost 16 hours of static abdominal holds

In for the Long Haul

Chilly Challenge

Clad only in swimming trunks, Jin Songhao endured 120 minutes immersed in a plastic box filled with ice. During the same year, the iceman from China's Heilongjiang Province also spent 46 minutes buried in snow, and took a bone-chilling shower by pouring 90 buckets of ice water over his head while standing on the frozen surface of the Songhua River.

Money Puzzle

A Chinese woman suffering from mental illness ripped up banknotes worth 50,000 yuan ($7,930), which her husband had saved for her medical treatment. He took the money to the bank where 12 of the workers spent six hours trying to piece the notes together, but they managed to salvage only one note in that time. When the bank couldn't help, a student suggested scanning the fragments and matching them up on a computer.

Pulling Their Weight

Eleven ex-soldiers climbed 3,209 feet to the peak of one of England's highest mountains with household appliances strapped to their backs. It took the group eight hours to carry the washing machines and dryers up and down the steep slopes of Scafell Pike. They were raising money to help wounded service members.

Think spot!

British couple Alex Pelling and Lisa Gant are planning their wedding in 30 different countries over three years. They will then marry officially in their favorite place.

Juggling Joe

Joe Salter juggled his way through a triathlon in April 2012, completing the course in less than two hours. He juggled constantly while swimming on his back for a quarter of a mile, biking 16.2 miles, and running four miles. The counselor from Pensacola, Florida, dropped a ball just three times during the swimming leg.

PROOF OF EVIDENCE

MAN OF MANY TALENTS

Thaneswar Guragai from Nepal spun a basketball on top of a toothbrush for 22½ seconds with the other end in his mouth. He can also pass his body through a tennis racket 38 times in one minute!

Wow!

FIVE-DAY DIVE

Scuba instructor Allen Sherrod spent 120 hours, 14 minutes, and 11 seconds beneath the waters of Lake David, Florida. He stayed on a pontoon boat 20 feet beneath the surface, where a support crew provided food through a tube.

Tower Stunt

Hezi Dean stood on top of a nine-story-high tower with no food for over 35 hours. A crane hoisted the Israeli endurance artist onto a small platform on the 89-foot structure in Tel Aviv. He dove into a pile of cardboard boxes at the end.

WATER BABY

Four-year-old Tae Smith from Dorset, England, swam 101 lengths of a pool—a distance of 1¼ miles—and stopped only when her instructor told her that she had done enough. She had been swimming for only five months.

SUPER-SIZED SHIRT

A giant T-shirt, unveiled in Nashville, Tennessee, in 2011, took six weeks to make and contained enough fabric to make 12,000 regular-sized shirts. The shirt was 281.3 feet long and 180.9 feet wide—almost as big as a football field—and weighed more than two tons.

DUCKS IN A ROW

In June 2011, over 80 volunteers arranged 17,782 yellow rubber ducks in a mile-long chain, which snaked its way through Warren G. Magnuson Park, Seattle, Washington.

TOP OF THE WORLD

George Atkinson climbed the highest mount on each continent at 16 as part of the Seven Summits challenge. The English schoolboy scaled Kilimanjaro, Mount Elbrus, Carstensz Pyramid, Mount Aconcagua, Mount McKinley, and Mount Vinson between 2005 and 2010. He finished on Mount Everest in May 2011.

Hi, Mom!

HIGH ACHIEVER

Most slackliners balance on nylon webbing close to the ground, but San Francisco resident Andy Lewis took the extreme sport to a new level by making a 45-foot crossing above a 100-foot-deep ravine in Flat Sands, California, without a safety net. As if that were not risky enough, he struck a pose for the camera by balancing on his ankles.

FIERY FEAT

Denni Düsterhöft ran 393.7 feet with his protective clothing ablaze, without the aid of oxygen, in November 2011. The German stuntman said he was exhausted after the challenge, known as the "Full Body Burn Run," because he could barely breathe.

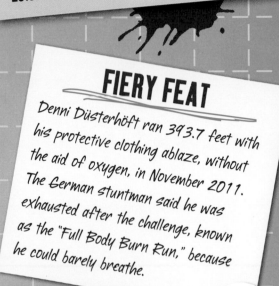

Bridezilla Alert

Emma Dumitrescu took to a hot-air balloon to show off a wedding-gown train 9,022 feet long. It took ten seamstresses from the Andree Salon fashion house 100 days to make the dress, which was displayed in Bucharest, Romania.

IN THE LION'S DEN

Alexander Pylyshenko lived in a cage with a lioness and her two cubs for 35 days. The private zoo owner and artist from the Ukraine slept on the floor and ate meat put through the bars. He painted pictures of the animals while he shared their living quarters, which he plans to sell for charity.

Can You Do This?

Card Sharp

Bai Dengchun can fling playing cards with such force that they slice through watermelons and cucumbers. The martial arts fan from northern China's Shandong Province can also burst balloons and break eggs by throwing cards. His skill earned him a place on *China's Got Talent*, where he cut through 12 cucumbers in less than 100 seconds.

Connecting Flight

Paul Steiner performed an incredible stunt by walking along the wing of a glider flying at 6,890 feet, then stepping onto a second glider that was flying underneath. The Austrian skydiver then stood on the fuselage of the second glider, while the first turned upside down and flew overhead. He reached up and grabbed its tail fin to form a link between the two aircraft.

What's unfolding?

Flick to page 126 to see more!

Bench Balancer

Li Hongxiao held 23 benches with his teeth for 11 seconds. The 30-year-old from southwest China has been balancing objects in his mouth since he was a child. With each three-foot-long bench weighing 6.6 pounds, the weight of this unsteady load totaled 152 pounds—almost equal to his bodyweight.

Think spot!

Arnold Erlandson from Gary, Indiana, accidentally swallowed a tack. Unbelievably, two years later, it had moved to his wrist —and was removed.

Mmmm, tasty!

Jaw-Dropping Stunt

Liu Fei from Jiangxi Province, China, slides three-foot-long live cauliflower snakes up his nostrils and lets them emerge through his mouth. Although the snakes are not venomous, Liu has had a few accidents with the wriggly reptiles, and once swallowed one.

Fighting the Elements

Against the Odds

On Christmas Eve 1971, the plane Juliane Koepcke was flying in was hit by lightning and exploded two miles above the Peruvian rain forest. Miraculously, Juliane was thrown outside and, still strapped to her chair, crashed through the rain forest canopy to the forest floor. Breaking only her collarbone and her glasses, she managed to find a small stream close to the crash and waded downstream for nine days—feeling her way, since she couldn't see without glasses. All she had to eat was a bag of candy she found on the plane, but she managed to stay hydrated by drinking the freshwater from the stream. Using the skills her father, a biologist, had taught her, she survived insect bites and infection, until she finally came across forest workers who helped her.

Going Off-Road

Free skier Tomas Bergemalm successfully completed a 600-foot cliff jump in Chamonix, France. The Swedish daredevil, who first took to the slopes at the age of 15, decided to attempt the breathtaking stunt as one of his last challenges before spending more time with his family.

Think spot!

Mark Inglis lost both legs to frostbite after a disastrous climb in New Zealand. He later climbed Mount Everest with prosthetic limbs.

Snow Survivor

A 44-year-old Swedish man survived for two months after becoming trapped in his car in the north of the country. It is thought that the snow covering the car acted like an igloo as temperatures fell to −22°F, and Peter Skyllberg was saved by his warm clothes and sleeping bag. He ate nothing but snow and lost more than 40 pounds during his ordeal.

Public Transport

Junkyard Bots

It looks like a character from a *Transformers* movie but "Scrap Metal Hercules" is made from recycled bulldozers, fire extinguishers, and old tires. Artist Zhu Kefeng and his team have spent ten years building giant metal robots from recycled parts. Their scrap metal masterpieces are now on display in a robot-themed outdoor gallery in China's Zhejiang Province.

Walk in the Park

Four architectural students from Dalhousie University created this grass-lined wheel to highlight the lack of green space in downtown Halifax, Canada. Not only can pedestrians enjoy the feel of grass beneath their feet, the hamster-style wheel will keep them dry when it's raining, too.

Gym Bus

For commuters who don't have time for the gym, Rio de Janeiro's Bus Bike offers a spinning class on wheels. The city bus is fitted with 16 stationary bikes, along with a dressing room, fridge, and sound system. Cyclists get the opportunity to ride the streets of Brazil's second-largest city and admire the views without having to keep an eye out for traffic.

Think spot!

John and Nancy Vogel and their sons, set out from Alaska in June 2008 to cycle the Pan-American Highway. They finished in Argentina in March 2011, after traveling 17,300 miles.

Off-Street Parking

When passersby saw a car balanced in an oak tree, they thought it might be a political statement or an art installation. In fact, it was the work of car enthusiast Gregan Thompson, who had taken the engine out of the three-wheeled Reliant Robin and decided to hoist the fiberglass shell into the tree in Preston Bagot, England, as a joke.

109

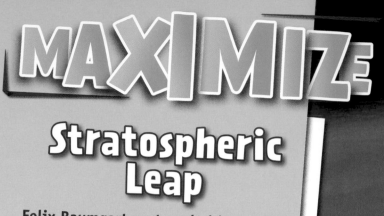

MAXIMIZE

Stratospheric Leap

Felix Baumgartner traveled into the stratosphere, 24 miles above the Earth, in a capsule carried by a huge helium balloon—then jumped out headfirst. His speed went from 0 to 833.9 mph as he plummeted toward Earth, and he was in free fall for four minutes and 19 seconds before opening his parachute and landing safely in the New Mexico desert. The Austrian skydiver had previously jumped from the Millau Viaduct in France, and the 101-story Taipei 101 in Taiwan, and plunged face-first into a 620-foot-deep cave in Croatia.

STRIKE A NOTE

✳ Felix traveled into the stratosphere where the temperature is around −60°F. The air is too thin to breathe there, and atmospheric pressure is roughly one-hundredth of what it is at sea level, which causes bubbles to form in the blood.

✳ The helium-filled balloon is made of 40 acres of plastic film—enough to wrap more than five million sandwiches. It is attached to a fireproof, pressurized capsule made of fiberglass. The capsule and balloon stand 764 feet high at launch, the equivalent of a 75-story building.

✳ Felix wore a high-tech cross between a sleeping bag and a close-fitting, pressurized spacesuit. This life-support system was his only protection until he reached the safer lower atmosphere.

✳ Two cylinders on his back supplied 100 percent oxygen through his helmet. Felix breathed this for two hours before the ascent to expel nitrogen from his body, which could cause decompression sickness, as the air gets thinner the higher you go.

Eccentric or Genius?

TEED UP

Balancing three golf balls on top of one another is difficult enough, but six-year-old Sol Hartman, pictured here in 1932, could hit each ball individually, without disturbing the one below.

ONE-MAN BAND

Don Tranger was able to play three trumpets at the same time in three-part harmony. He also played a clarinet and a saxophone simultaneously.

LIVING DANGEROUSLY

This performer at Barnum & Bailey Circus is demonstrating a bond of trust by placing himself inside an elephant's mouth. Any pressure from the creature's jaws could crush the man's skull.

GYM RAT

It's never too early to start exercising. Baby La Varace Anderson, photographed in 1935, could hold herself up on a pole and do chin-ups at the age of six months.

Putting on a performance that would be remarkable in a man a third of his age, retired US Marine Carl Richartz is shown holding himself horizontal on a vertical bar for 30 seconds at the age of 65. He was 61 when he first attempted the amazing feat.

POLE POSITION

Eighty-year-old A.T. Brown was photographed climbing, not only headfirst, but also backward, down a 40-foot-high telegraph pole during the 1930s.

HUMAN BRIDGE

Max Brenton, a professional wrestler and body builder, is shown here performing his strongman act in Nebraska, in 1924. Although he weighed just 140 pounds, he is holding three men, weighing a total of 616 pounds.

Risky Business

The lead is melted in a small furnace and transferred onto a spoon.

When the metal has solidified, Tim spits it out.

Going for the Burn

During the day, Tim Cockerill works at Britain's Cambridge University but, at night, the zoologist stuns audiences as "The Great Inferno." Inspired by a 1950s music hall act, Tim breathes fire, applies a blowtorch burning at 2,900°F to his tongue, and chews a spoonful of molten lead for 30 seconds until it solidifies. As a break from his exploits, he entertains the crowds by driving a power drill, or hammering long nails, into his nose.

INTERVIEW

● Tim, how do you even start to learn how to chew molten lead?
I can't tell you because fire-eaters have been performing this stunt for over 200 years and the technique is still a closely guarded secret. But I will tell you that it takes years of practice before you're ready to perform.

● Lead is toxic, the temperatures involved are immense, and the mouth is a sensitive place. Have you ever been injured?
This is a very dangerous stunt for lots of reasons. Luckily, I have never had a serious injury, but it took me many years of training until I was confident enough to try it. I do still get nervous when I'm about to perform it!

● What new stunts do you want to perform?
There was a famous fire-eater called Ivan Ivanitz Chabert who called himself "The Fire King." In 1826, he stepped into a giant oven holding a leg of lamb. When he came out, the leg of lamb was fully cooked but he was completely unharmed! If I could find an oven big enough I'd love to try it, and I do love roast lamb. . . .

Wheel Walk

High-wire artist Nik Wallenda, of the famed "Flying Wallendas" family, upped the stakes by walking on top of a turning Ferris wheel at the Santa Cruz Beach Boardwalk, California. Nik has been stunt walking since age four, and never relies on a safety net. He even proposed to his wife, Erendira, 30 feet in the air.

Electric Performance

Australian-born Chayne Hultgren started practicing the death-defying art of sword-swallowing at the age of 16, using a garden hose. Since then, he has graduated to swallowing multiple swords, table legs, and, now, neon tubes powered by 2,000 volts of electricity that can be seen glowing inside his body. The fragile glass tubes contain deadly mercury gas.

Curious Exploits

Massive Mouth

Zhang Dong makes a living from his huge mouth. The 29-year-old from Liaoning, China, can fit six ceramic Chinese soup spoons into his mouth—sideways. He uses this strange skill to entertain tourists and locals, and even auditioned for *China's Got Talent*.

RIPLEY RECORDS

▶ **LONGEST SURVIVAL WITHOUT FOOD** Angus Barbieri from Scotland lived only on water, seltzer, tea, coffee, and vitamins from June 1965 to July 1966.

▶ **WEIGHT LIFTED BY TONGUE** Thomas Blackthorne from the UK can lift a 27 pound 8.96 ounce weight suspended from a hook through his tongue.

▶ **SPEEDY CONTORTIONIST** Skye Broberg takes only 4.78 seconds to squeeze herself into a box just 20.4 x 17.7 x 17.7 inches.

▶ **MOST TATTOOED WOMAN** American Cynthia J. Martell had tattoos covering 96 percent of her body—except her palms and the soles of her feet.

Elfin Features

Movies such as the *Lord of the Rings* and *Avatar* have sparked a trend for elflike ears among some extreme fans. Kimberleigh Roseblade from Vancouver, Canada, regularly wore prosthetic elf ears until body-modification artist Russ Foxx sculpted her real ears into pixie points.

Handy Man

Su Yongbo works as a security guard, but he would surely be welcome on any building site. The 17-year-old from Xian, Shaanxi Province, China, can carry eight bricks in one hand. The total weight of this giant handful is around 40 pounds.

Bristling Beard

George Gaspar from Sherman Oaks, California, spent 90 minutes sticking 2,222 toothpicks into his beard. It took George 1½ years to grow his epic facial hair, which he shampoos and conditions daily. He is a proud member of Beard Team USA, and has competed in the World Beard and Mustache Championships.

Performing Art

chapter 6

Kids' Play

Toy Town

A disused railway bridge in Wuppertal, Germany, is giving drivers something to talk about. Street artist Megx sought permission to transform the structure's drab concrete, then spent four weeks painstakingly painting it to look like it's made entirely of LEGO® bricks.

What's unfolding?

Flick to page 72 to see more!

Think spot!

Barbie's full name is Barbara Millicent Roberts. The daughter of Barbie's creator was named Barbara.

Pi-Zzz-a Pie

Perfect for sleepovers, these handmade, pizza-slice sleeping bags come with a choice of toppings, including broccoli, mushrooms, or olives, supplied as bag decorations or extra pillows. Each bag is lined with satin, and sleepers can rest their heads on a stuffed crust bolster. Pizza-loving textile artist Brook Abboud produces the bags to order.

Barbie Bling

Brooklyn artist Margaux Lange turns deconstructed Barbie dolls into quirky jewelry. Combined with sterling silver and pigmented resins, arms become necklaces, ears are turned into earrings, eyes wink out from rings, and multiple mouths smile from pendants. Ken is not forgotten—his six-pack abs are displayed on neck chains and rings.

Going Down?

Unsuspecting shoppers in a London, UK, mall got a shock when the doors of the elevator opened to reveal a deep, bottomless shaft. They soon discovered it was an illusion set up by a theme park to test out the British public's levels of fear in preparation for the launch of a new ride. Artist Andrew Walker created the 3-D illusion on the floor of the elevator.

Face Facts

Fiery Head

The first time one of David Mach's sculptures got set alight, it was an unwelcome accident, to say the least, but now no sooner has he finished one of his artworks than he deliberately adds a flame. His impressive portraits of everyone from Elvis to Betty Boop are made from hundreds of different-colored matches meticulously stuck into fiberglass models. When the matches light, "You don't lose the portrait. You just get something different," he says.

Face Fusion

People from around the world have participated in the Internet craze of "moneyfacing." Banknotes are folded to show half the portrait and strategically placed in front of people's faces. A man might use a five-dollar bill to give himself Abraham Lincoln's beard, or a woman could make it look as if she is wearing the British Queen's crown.

The Toastman

New Zealander Maurice Bennett creates billboard-size portraits using slices of toast. His subjects include the *Mona Lisa*, Elvis Presley, and Barack Obama. Each portrait requires thousands of slices of bread, toasted using a blowtorch and a cast-iron stencil to create highlights and shadows. Once a work is complete, it is preserved with a coat of polyurethane.

Crafty Craftwork

Fabric of History

Alexi Torres's portraits look handwoven and 3-D, but in fact the intricate patterns have been painstakingly painted. The Cuban-born artist, now based in Atlanta, Georgia, works on five canvases at a time, and each takes between six and eight weeks to complete. He sees his work as representing the weaving of incidents in history and their effect on one another.

Knitted Graffiti

A mystery "yarnbomber" struck in Saltburn, England, just before the 2012 Olympics, and wrapped a 150-foot Olympic-themed scarf around the railings of the town's historic pier. The scarf featured woolen athletes, from swimmers to cyclists. A scarf with knitted books on it was previously left outside the library, presumably by the same anonymous creator.

Stitch Up

Polish-born Agata Oleksiak takes everyday objects, such as household goods, vehicles, and public sculptures, and transforms them with a covering of crocheted yarn. Life and art are inseparable for the artist, now based in New York, and anything that enters her world will be highlighted in wool. Even text messages are immortalized as crocheted panels.

RIPLEY RECORDS

▶ **FASTEST TATTOOIST** Pavan Ahluwalia from the UK completed 511 henna armband tattoos in an hour.

▶ **MOST DEDICATED SEAMSTRESS** Heather Hems from the UK spent 12 hours every day for 17 years creating a piece of embroidery the size of 12 table tennis tables.

▶ **MOST CRYSTALS ON A WEDDING DRESS** Özden Gelinlik Moda Tasarim Ltd, a Turkish firm, sewed 45,024 crystals onto a single wedding gown in five days.

▶ **TALLEST MOHAWK** Kazuhiro Watanabe from Japan fashions his long locks into a towering 44.6-inch Mohawk that tapers to a spike.

Hair Style

This 0.8 x 1.2-inch portrait is made of woven hair! Chinese artist Zhang Dexuan used 300 hairs and took two months to complete the picture. "You have to have a peaceful mind," he says, "as even normal breath will blow the job away." According to Zhang, it took him 54 years to acquire the skills of hair weaving, which he learned from his parents.

Body Work

Ewwww!

British artists Mariana Fantich and Dominic Young have given the Barker Oxfords shoe a gruesome makeover by replacing the soles with 1,050 teeth. But don't be alarmed—the teeth on the soles of these shoes are definitely plastic dentures, not human teeth!

Movie Manicures

Kayleigh O'Connor decorates her nails with popular film, television, and cartoon characters, spending up to two hours on each themed design. Her tribute to the 1975 movie *Jaws* features a shark on her thumb and a terrified swimmer on her ring finger. Thumbnails have also been transformed into Kermit the Frog and a whole scene from *Up*—complete with floating house and a balloon.

Thumb-One Famous?

When Italian artist Dito Von Tease was looking for an original avatar to use as his profile picture on Facebook, he came up with the idea of using a dressed-up finger version of himself. Now he's applied the same technique to famous faces, digitally enhancing his painted fingers, adding hairstyles, clothes, and features, to re-create everyone from Hello Kitty and Shrek to Neytiri from *Avatar* and Waldo from *Where's Waldo?*

Think spot!

Robert Norton Kennedy from South Carolina had a tattoo on his forehead that read, "Please forgive me if I say or do anything stupid. Thank you!"

Head Lines

This man, spotted at Bike Week 2012 in Daytona Beach, Florida, certainly feels the need for eyes in the back of his head. Not only has he had a whole face tattooed on the back of his head, but he's even left patches of hair on his mostly-shaved crown to provide eyebrows and a long mustache.

127

PROOF OF EVIDENCE

BIG BOOM

A drum kit 21.3 feet tall and 26.25 feet wide was set up in Vienna's Prater Luna Park for Austria's May Day celebrations in 2012. Four drummers played the giant instruments.

MARATHON SESSION

In 2011, Dave Browne played the guitar continuously for 114 hours, 6 minutes, and 30 seconds in a Dublin pub. The Irish musician took a 30-second break between songs and a 40-minute break every eight hours to nap, eat, shower, and change. He played 1,372 different pieces of music—an average of 12 an

BRIDAL SWEETS

Top British wedding designers got together with a confectionery company to produce bridal wear decorated with candy in celebration of the Queen's Diamond Jubilee in 2012. Designs included a wedding dress covered in marshmallows.

CAPED CRUSADER

The Brazilian city of Taubaté has hired a 50-year-old military veteran to dress up as Batman. Police and residents hope that Andre Luiz Pinheiro will inspire others to help clean up the neighborhood, and talk to children in troubled areas about crime.

MULTICOLORED MAKEOVER

Fashion designer Matthew Williamson teamed up with a leading paint manufacturer to turn dull areas into colorful communities. The Ravensbourne Community Centre in London was the first UK project, and local volunteers transformed the building into a striking, rainbow-patterned landmark.

WIZARD WEAR AND TEAR

Daniel Radcliffe, who played Harry Potter, went through 70 wands and 160 pairs of glasses during the filming of all eight movies.

amooosing

MILKING IT

British comedian Milton Jones performed a stand-up routine to a field of cows to test their reactions. His jokes, written especially for the gig, included, "You cows say you're vegetarians—but how come you all wear leather?"

PYROTECHNIC PAINTER

New York artist Rosemarie Fiore creates abstract artworks by exploding fireworks on paper. She uses color smoke bombs, fountains, and other fireworks, controlling the explosions in upside-down containers.

ARTISTIC PRODIGY

Aelita Andre from Melbourne, Australia, began painting before she could walk. Recognizing her talent, her parents submitted her work to a gallery. The gallery arranged an exhibition for her, not realizing she was only two years old.

AGAINST THE ODDS

Because of a birth defect that stunted the growth of her arms, Zohreh Etezad Saltaneh has to do everything with her feet. Her mother put a paintbrush between her toes at an early age and now her artwork has been exhibited around the world. The Iranian artist also weaves, sends text messages, and carries out household chores with her feet.

LATEST ACCESSORY

A company based in London, England, is producing artificial animal tails for humans, which attach to the body with an elasticized waistband. People who feel that their tailbones are missing a tail can choose from fox, lemur, lizard, squirrel, lion, or dinosaur.

Home Is Where the Art Is

Spot On

Japanese artist Yayoi Kusama constructed a totally white living space for Australia's Queensland Gallery of Modern Art, then invited thousands of the museum's youngest visitors to transform the installation with colored stickers. After two weeks, the kids had wreaked multicolored mayhem, and the height of some of the stickers proves that adults joined in the fun, too.

Suitable for Vegetarians

This is Vicky McDonald's sweet take on the traditional English breakfast. The Irish food blogger used peanut butter sponge cake to create the sausage, and the egg is panna cotta with a lemon curd yolk. The bacon is made from wafers, the blood sausage is chocolate cookie cake, the hash brown is made from brioche, and the baked beans are homemade cookies in a fruit sauce.

Gathering Dust

Before Allison Cortson starts work on a portrait, she asks her subject for several months' worth of vacuum cleaner bags. The Californian artist uses the dust to create the background to her paintings and says it is the perfect material because, as dust is partly human skin, it has been produced by the person in the picture.

Aaa-chooo!

Think spot!

People with Stendhal Syndrome suffer from fainting, confusion, and even hallucinations when they see great works of art.

On a Roll

Entries in the Scotch Tape contest prove that you can produce art from materials sitting right on your desk. The company set customers the challenge of creating sculptures with rolls of the sticky tape. Tania B. from Cape Coral, Florida, used six rolls of tape to make this model of a dog, named *Come Play With Me*.

Clever Costumes

Collapsible Hat

Photographed by the River Seine in Paris, France, in 1954, this woman is wearing a hat with an inflatable brim, which her friend is helping to inflate. The design meant it could be deflated and folded up in a bag, or put in a pocket. At least it would have floated if it had blown off and landed in the river!

Great or Gross?

Curious about some people's dislike of cut hair, British student Kerry Howley created a collection of necklaces made from human hair to try to make discarded hair attractive. The five ornate necklaces each took over 60 hours to make and were part of her graduate collection called "Attraction/Aversion."

Definitely gross!

Height of Fashion

Models from Boston's Rock Gym rappelled down a vertical catwalk to celebrate the opening of a new hotel. Some even performed spectacular swan dives to the delight of spectators, who watched the action through free binoculars. They were modeling the hotel's uniforms, designed by students at the Massachusetts College of Art and Design, and clothes from the UK design company Ted Baker.

Human Chameleon

Sculptor and artist Cecilia Paredes likes to lose herself in her work. Using body paint, makeup, and costumes, the queen of camouflage blends seamlessly into her bold wallpaper backgrounds. The artist, who relocated from Peru to Costa Rica, then to Philadelphia, Pennsylvania, sees her work as a symbol of how she has had to adjust in order to fit in.

I'm here!

What's unfolding? Flick to page 59 to see more!

MAXIMIZE

Celebrity Circles

Belgian artist Ben Heine creates portraits of celebrities from thousands of colored circles. He uses a sharp, round brush in Photoshop and calls the technique "Digital Circlism." Each circle is a different size, color, and tone, and is applied individually to a black background. The process is time-consuming and portraits can take up to nine days to complete. His subjects include Lady Gaga, Eminem, Elvis Presley, Marilyn Monroe, and Freddie Mercury.

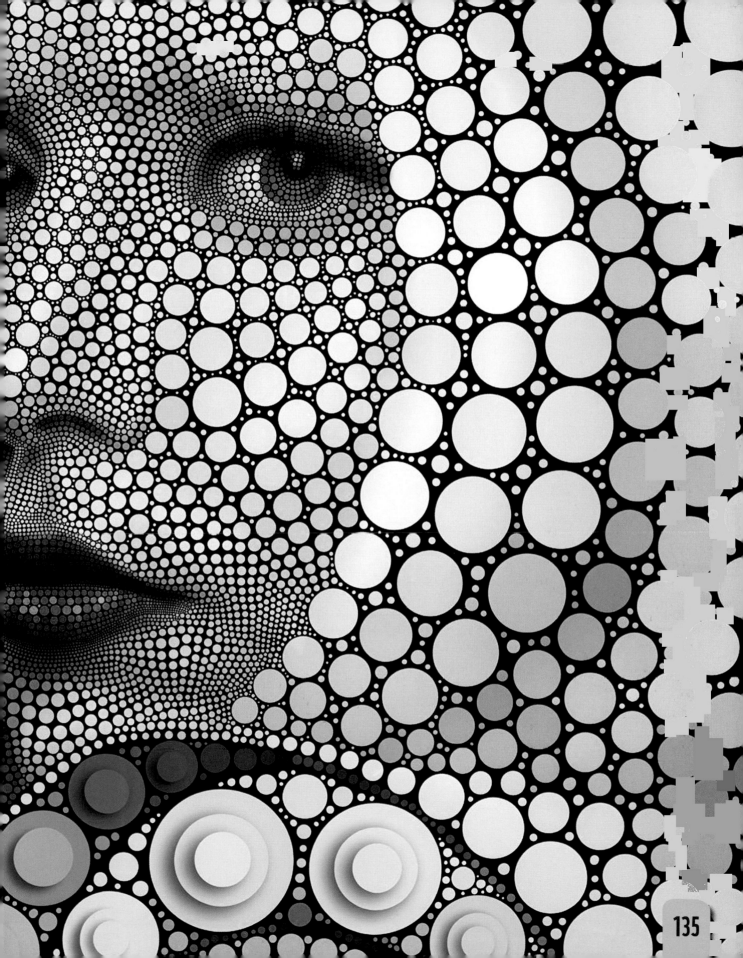

Lights, Camera, Action!

Great Shot!

Alan Sailer's high-speed photograph captures the moment a pellet fired from an air rifle hits an egg. The amateur photographer, who is based in California, made his own high-speed flash, which is triggered as the pellet passes through a laser beam. The flash of light lasts around a millionth of a second, allowing him to freeze images such as this that we would otherwise never see.

EGGSPLODE!

Daddy!

Open Wide

Pinhole camera expert Justin Quinnell from England placed one of his cameras in his mouth and took photographs of everything from his young son to the Sydney Opera House. Sometimes he had to stand completely still with his mouth wide open for up to a minute for the film to be properly exposed. He even filmed his visit to the dentist.

Making a Splash

Jack Long from Milwaukee, Wisconsin, produced these floral pictures using paint—but no brushes or canvases were involved. Armed instead with a high-speed camera and infinite patience, the artist created *Vessels and Blooms*, a series of photographs of splashing liquids that resemble flowers in vases. He used an electronic flash to capture the split second when the droplets of paint were suspended in the air, and did not resort to any computer trickery apart from cleaning up the images.

Think spot!

Artist Erik Kessels printed out a million photos to represent the number that are uploaded to Flickr in 24 hours—and piled them up in one room.

Happy Mediums

Lovely Bones

LA artist Darren Pearson heads for skate parks, beaches, and campsites to create his glow-in-the-dark skeletons. He opens his camera shutter and for seven minutes draws his designs in the air using a light. He can't see what he's drawing in front of him, but the camera captures the light trails, which show up as shimmering lines in the final image.

Think Spot!

An artist from Chicago named Dwight Kalb created a statue of Madonna using 180 pounds of ham.

Crafty Cooking

You'd be forgiven for reaching out for a needle and thread, but this particular sewing box is really a cake! Every button and pin is edible and is the delicate work of British Meg Davis.

Glittering Critters

Gardeners often hang old CDs around their vegetable gardens because the shiny surfaces scare birds. However, Sean Avery's recycled CD sculptures of a predatory cat or a peregrine falcon would be far more effective. The Australian artist creates his glinting menagerie by gluing CD shards to a wire mesh frame. They take up to three months to complete and some contain over 1,000 disks.

STRIKE A NOTE

✳ In 1961, Matisse's painting *Le Bateau* hung upside down in New York's Museum of Modern Art for 47 days before anyone noticed.

✳ Mount Rushmore is one of the largest sculptures in the world. The heads of the four US presidents, carved into the Black Hills, South Dakota, are 16 feet tall. If their bodies had been carved as well, each man would have stood 465 feet tall.

✳ Vincent van Gogh's *Portrait of Dr. Gachet* fetched a record price of $82.5 million when sold at auction in New York in 1990, but the artist only sold one painting, *Red Vineyard at Arles*, during his lifetime for the equivalent of only $1,600.

Food for Thought

UK butcher Anthony Dunphy has turned his work into an art form by using meat in his paintings! He combines gloss paint with boiled lamb and chicken bones to create four-foot-tall artworks—such as this portrait of soccer player David Beckham—which he says are inspired by pop art pioneer Andy Warhol.

Photo Credits

Ripley Entertainment Inc. and the editors of this book wish to thank the following photographers, agents, and other individuals for permission to use and reprint the following photographs in this book. Any photographs included in this book that are not acknowledged below are property of the Ripley Archives. Great effort has been made to obtain permission from the owners of all material included in this book. Any errors that may have been made are unintentional and will gladly be corrected in future printings if notice is sent to Ripley Entertainment Inc., 7576 Kingspointe Parkway, Suite 188, Orlando, Florida 32819.

COVER: China Foto Press/Photocome/Press Association Images

BACK COVER: Clockwise: Two-faced cat—Andrew Cunningham, Cummings School of Veterenary Medicine, Tufts University; Tech shoes—Marianna Fanzich and Dominic Young; Juggling swimming—Flora Bama Lounge Perdido Key, FL

CONTENTS PAGES: 2: Crochet car—Courtesy of Olek; Sword swallowing—The Space Cowboy; Digital head—Taras Lesko (www.visualspicer.com); **3:** CD bird—Sean E. Avery; Two-faced cat—Andrew Cunningham, Cummings School of Veterinary Medicine, Tufts University; Teeth shoes—Mariana Fantich and Dominic Young

INTRO PAGES: 7: Goats in tree—Gavin Oliver/Solent News/Rex Features; Russian daredevils—Alexander Remnev/Solent News/Rex Features

CHAPTER 1: 10: White rainbow—© Caters News Agency; Ice Chandeliers—Patrick Pleul/DPA/Press Association Images; Background—Tuna SARIKAYA—Shutterstock.com *(and throughout)*; **11:** Indoor clouds—Berndnaut Smilde Nimbus ll 2012 Photo: Cassander Eeftinck Schattenkerk; Lenticular cloud—Magrath/Folsom/Science Photo Library; Think spot—Lunarus—Shutterstock.com *(and throughout)*; **12:** Blue water—© Photoshot; GPS art drawing—Dallas Childers/Rex Features; GPS art map—Michael Wallace/Rex Features; **13:** Pink tree—Ben Birchall/PA Wire/Press Association Images; Street art—Nikita Nomerz/Rex Features; What's unfolding—Chris Van Wyk; **14:** Kayaking on waterfall edge—Desré Tate; **15:** Cooking on volcano—© Kristjan Logason/Demotix/Demotix/Demotix/Corbis; Ice hotel—Reuters/Radu Sigheti; **16:** Camera clothes—Tyler Card/Rex Features; Bottled air—KeystoneUSA-ZUMA/Rex Features; **17:** Big deckchair—Chris Ison/PA Wire/Press Association Images; Hen predicts weather—Solent News/Rex Features; **18–19:** Paper—Nenov Brothers Photography—Shutterstock.com *(and throughout)*; Pushpin paper—sergign—Shutterstock.com *(and throughout)*; Cutting mat background—takito—Shutterstock.com *(and throughout)*; **18:** Wave—Zacarias Pereira da Mata—Shutterstock.com; Snake—Eric Isselee—Shutterstock.com; **19:** Boarding passes—Sashkin—Shutterstock.com; Christmas star—Sayko—Shutterstock.com; **20:** Swimming with jellyfish—© Caters News Agency; Boat sinking—www.julienberthier.org courtesy galerie GP&N Vallois, Paris; **21:** Ice caves—© Caters News Agency; Hanging hot tub—Sébastien Martinet/SWNS.com; What's unfolding—The Space Cowboy; **22:** Pylons—© Choi+Shine; Flying saucer hotel—© Caters News Agency; **23:** Lockheed—Courtesy of Lockheed Martin; **24:** Salt ponds—Jerry Ting; Toilet waterfall—© Photoshot; **25:** Skull lake—Andrew Price/Rex Features; Earth in a droplet—Markus Reugels/Rex Features; **26–27:** Volcano man—Carsten Peter/National Geographic Stock; **28:** Longest washing line—© Patrick Seeger/epa/Corbis; Hangar home—Courtesy of Joe Pires; **29:** Boat shopping centre—© Victor Fraile/Corbis; What's unfolding—Courtesy of Kimberleigh Smithbower Roseblade; Monster Motorbike—Reuters/Sukree Sukplang

CHAPTER 2: 32: Dean Gunnarson—Canadian Press/Rex Features; **33:** Ferris wheel plane crash—AAP Image/Press Association Images; Boy stuck in air conditioning unit—Quirky China News/Rex Features; **34:** Very cold woman—TPG/AP/Press Association Images; Gurner—ChinaFotoPress/Photocome/Press Association Image; **35:** Bendy arm man—Hai yang/Imaginechina; Contortionist—Reuters/China Photos; **36:** Eating spider—© Heng Sinith/epa/Corbis; Lizards on sticks—© Photoshot; **37:** Ducks tongues—Reuters/Paul Yeung; Chocolate boat—© Photoshot; What's unfolding—Taras Lesko (www.visualspicer.com); **38:** Cockroaches—Somchai Som—Shutterstock.com; Giant ear—Birgit Reitz-Hofmann—Shutterstock.com; **39:** Fork—AlenKadr—Shutterstock.com; Mount Everest—Pal Teravagimov—Shutterstock.com; **42:** Big family—Richard Grange/Barcroft India; Soccer team with the same name—© Albanpix.ltd; **43:** Blonde-haired children—Sean Myles; **44:** Swimming moon lake—Udndata/Imaginechina; **45:** Escaping the desert on a motorbike—Emile Leray/Rex Features; Kids riding sheep—Mike Vogt/AP/Press Association Images; **46–47:** Smashing bricks with head—© Jeff J Mitchell/Reuters/Corbis; **48:** Sweeping bridge—Quirky China News/Rex Features; Russian daredevils—Alexander Remnev/Solent News/Rex Features; **49:** Cable car climb—© Caters News Agency; Glacier boarding—© Caters News Agency; **50:** Connie Tibbs—Laurentiu Garofeanu/Barcroft USA; **51:** Bull leaps into water—Fernando Bustamante/AP/Press Association Images; Giraffe Manor—Robin D. Moore/National Geographic Stock; What's unfolding—Courtesy of Olek

CHAPTER 3: 54: Goats in tree—Gavin Oliver/Solent News/Rex Features; Giant flamingo—Bobby Haas/National Geographic Stock; **55:** Chipmunk drinking—Mike Walker/Rex Features; Orphaned owls in cups—BNPS.co.uk; **56:** Cyclops shark—Pisces Sportfishing Fleet/Rex Features; Horse with a mustache—SWNS.com; **57:** Pink dolphin—© Caters News Agency/Rex Features; Tree shaped like a hippo—BNPS.co.uk; **58:** Kitten stuck in car engine—Matt Roper; **59:** Dog covered in porcupine quills—Sipa USA/Rex Features; Goats stuck on bridge—Sandra Church/Rimrock Humane Society; **60–61:** Spiderwebs—Reuters/Daniel Munoz; **62:** Elvis bug—© Caters News Agency; Duck in diaper—© Photoshot; **63:** Dog painted like tiger—© Photoshot; Mary River turtle—Chris Van Wyk; What's unfolding—www.julienberthier.org courtesy galerie GP&N Vallois, Paris; **64:** Stair lifts for dogs—Rex Features; Cat stuck in jar—www.sell-my-photo.co.uk; **65:** Chickens and iPads—SWNS.com; Elk saves marmot—© Caters News Agency; **66:** Turbot—BNPS.co.uk; Giant croc—Reuters/Stringer Philippines; **67:** Shrek the sheep after—AFP/Getty Images; Shrek the sheep before—Reuters/Simon Baker; **68:** Swan—E. O.—Shutterstock.com; Tractor—PRILL—Shutterstock.com; **69:** Washing machine—Fotocrisis—Shutterstock.com; **70:** Diving horse—Barcroft Media via Getty Images; Budgie that knows his way home—AP/Press Association Images; **71:** Cat on Twitter—Marc de Vinck/Rex Features; Seal in dinghy—Peter Mackley; **72:** Baby orange gorilla—London News Pictures/Rex Features; Two-faced cat—Andrew Cunningham, Cummings School of Veterinary Medicine, Tufts University; **73:** Calf with long tail—Jennifer Showalter; Camouflaged gecko—© Thomas Marent/Ardea.com

CHAPTER 4: 76: Room projector—Mr Beam/Rex Features; Digital head—Taras Lesko (www.visualspicer.com); **77:** Keyboard trousers—© Caters News Agency; Celebrity portraits—© Caters News Agency; **78:** Petri art—Zachary Copfer; **79:** Decaying food—© Caters News Agency; Clothes made of wine—Ray Scott/Rex Features; **80:** Tooth tattoos—Frank Wojciechowski/Rex Features; Chocolate brain—Inition/Rex Features; **81:** Woman who aged after seafood—© HotSpot Media; **82:** Marbles from space—Bournemouth News/Rex Features; Creature in road—Jeff Greenhaw/AP/Press Association Images; **83:** 3-D image of man—Human Media Lab/Rex Features; Cloud shaped like the UK—Dawn Melville/Rex Features; **84–85:** Own planets—Alexandre Duret-Lutz/Rex Features; **86:** Glow-in-the-dark jeans—Naked & Famous Denim/Rex Features; Sushi iPhone cover—Strapya/Rex Features; **87:** Interactive display car—Reuters/Kim Kyung-Hoon; Foldboat—© Arno Mathies & Max Frommeld; What's unfolding—Sean E. Avery; **88:** Albert Einstein in mountain—Rex Features; Harvestmen close up—Dr. Siwanowicz winner of the 2010 Olympus BioScapes Digital Imaging Competition. To see more amazing images, visit www.olympusbioscapes.com; **89:** World's smallest film—© Nokia 2010; Tim Noble reflective art—Blain Southern/Peter Mallet/Solent; **90:** David Blaine—Lynn Goldsmith/Rex Features; Giant eye—Reuters/handout; **91:** Space shuttle through streets—Getty Images; Woman who is afraid of buttons—M&Y Media/Rex Features; **92:** Puppy—WilleeCole—Shutterstock.com; **93:** Fish—Iakov Filimonov—Shutterstock.com; Cupcake—Ruth Black—Shutterstock.com; **94:** Man who sees in black and white—Michele Souza/DPA/Press Association Images; Converting breath to electricity—João Lammoglia/Rex Features; **95:** Bionic eye—Oxford Eye Hospital

CHAPTER 5: 98: Gary Connery jump—Getty Images; **99:** Surfing accident—© Caters News Agency; Crack climbers—© Caters News Agency; **100:** Man sitting on ice—© Xinhua/Photoshot; Shredded money—Nie wu/Imaginechina; **101:** Climbing with washing machines—Tim Stewart News/Rex Features; Juggling cycling and running—Jeff Nelson Studios; Juggling swimming—Flora Bama Lounge Perdido Key, FL; **102:** Scuba diver—marcogarrincha—Shutterstock.com; **103:** Mount Kilimanjaro—Oleg Znamenskiy—Shutterstock.com; Lion yawning—Elisabete—Shutterstock.com; **104:** Flicking cards into melon—Liu chang qd/Imaginechina; Holding onto two planes—© Europics; What's unfolding—Mariana Fantich and Dominic Young; **105:** Holding benches with teeth—© Photoshot; Snake in nose—ChinaFotoPress/Photocome/Press Association Images; **106:** Plane crash—AP/AP/Press Association Images; Rain forest—ODM—Shutterstock.com; **107:** Cliff jump—© Caters News Agency; Snowed in car—© Erik Astrom/Scanpix/Press Association Images; **108:** Hercules made out of JCBs—Wenn.com; Grass wheel—Wenn.com; **109:** Bus bike—Wenn.com; Car stuck in tree—© HotSpot Media; **110–111:** Felix Baumgartner—Getty Images; **114:** Tim Cockerill—Alex Smith/www.as-images.com; **115:** Nik Wallenda—Donaven Staab, Santa Cruz Beach Boardwalk; Space Cowboy—The Space Cowboy; **116:** Spoons in mouth—Wenn.com; Pixie ears—Courtesy of Kimberleigh Smithbower Roseblade; **117:** Holding bricks with one hand—© Photoshot; Toothpicks in beard—Wenn.com

CHAPTER 6: 120: LEGO® bridge—Rolf Dellenbusch/Rex Features; Pizza slice sleeping bag—Brook Abboud/Solent News/Rex Features; What's unfolding—Andrew Cunningham, Cummings School of Veterinary Medicine, Tufts University; **121:** Barbie jewelry—margauxlange.com/Solent News/Rex Features; Lift illusion—Rex Features; **122:** Matchstick devil—Steve Black/Rex Features; **123:** Banknote face—Solent News/Rex Features; Toast art—Shanghai Daily/Imaginechina; **124:** Alex Torres woven art—Alexi Torres/Rex Features; Olympic knitting—London News Pictures/Rex Features; **125:** Crochet car—Courtesy of Olek; Hair weaving art—Quirky China News/Rex Features; **126:** Shoes with false teeth—Mariana Fantich and Dominic Young; Nail tribute—Kayleigh O'Connor/Solent News/Rex Features; **127:** Finger art—Dito Von Tease/ditology.blogspot.com; Face tattooed on head—© Robert Caston/Demotix/Corbis; **128:** Heart—Oliko—Shutterstock.com; Guitar—A'lya—Shutterstock.com; **129:** Cow—smereka—Shutterstock.com; Purple foot—paul prescott—Shutterstock.com; Orange tag—Thinglass—Shutterstock.com; **130:** Sticker room art—Yayoi Kusama Installation view of The Obliteration Room 2002-present Commissioned Queensland Art Gallery. Gift of the artist through the Queensland Art Gallery Foundation 2012 Collection: Queensland Art Gallery, Australia © Yayoi Kusama, Yayoi Kusama Studio Inc. Photograph: Natasha Harth, QAGOMA; Breakfast made of cake—Stasty/Rex Features; **131:** Dust painting—Allison Cortson/Solent News/Rex Features; Scotch tape dog—Solent News/Rex Features; **132:** Blow-up hat—Barratts/S&G Barratts/EMPICS Archive; Hair jewelry Kerry Howley/Rex Features; **133:** Vertical catwalk—Dominick Reuter/EPA; Body camouflage—Cecilia Paredes/Rex Features; **134–135:** Lady Gaga pixel art—Ben Heine/Rex Features; **136:** Egg exploding—Alan Sailer/Rex Features; Camera in mouth—*Louis (getting to know dad)* Pinhole image by Justin Quinnell; **137:** Paint flower—Jack Long/Solent News; **138:** Skeleton light painting—Darren Pearson/Solent News; Sewing box made of cake—Apex; **139:** Falcon made of CDs—Sean E. Avery; Butcher art of David Beckham—Anthony Dunphy, artist, anthonyartwork@hotmail.co.uk/Nick Morgan @ ME5H/Cut Media

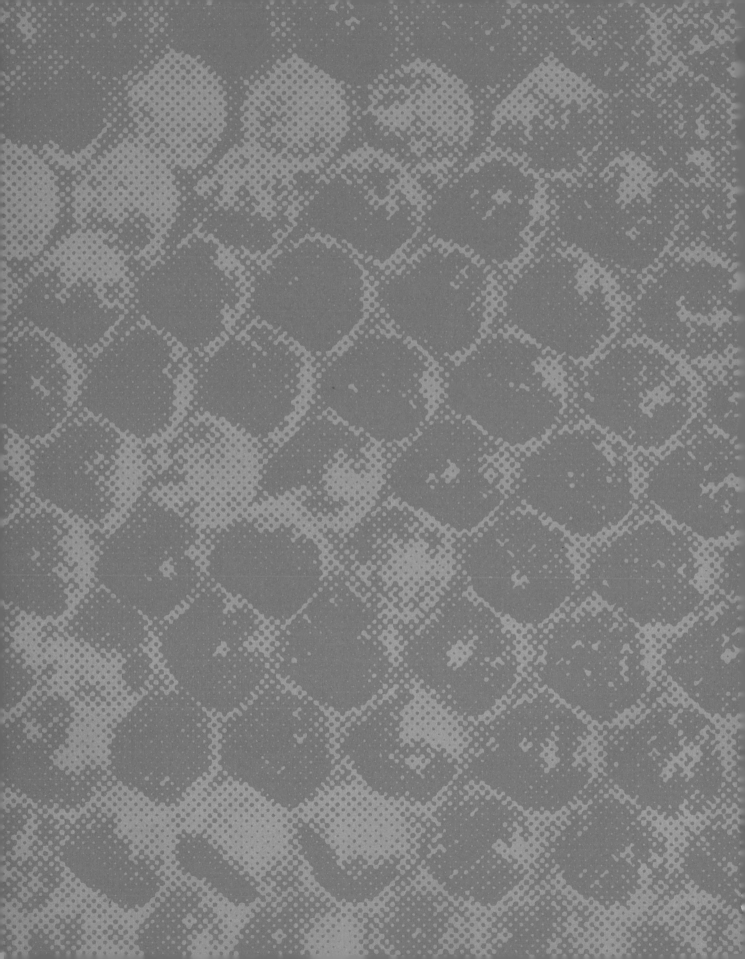